Andrea Seiger

111 Places
in Washington
That You
Must Not Miss

Photographs by John Dean

T0243779

emons:

For Mom & Dad who gave me the gifts of travel and curiosity, and for Chris who was always game for an adventure

Bibliographical information of the Deutsche Nationalbibliothek
The Deutsche Nationalbibliothek lists this publication in the Deutsche Nationalbibliografie; detailed bibliographical data are available on the internet at http://dnb.d-nb.de.

© Emons Verlag GmbH
All rights reserved
All photos © John Dean, except see page 239
© Cover motif: shutterstock.com/J Main
Layout: Eva Kraskes, based on a design
by Lübbeke | Naumann | Thoben
Edited by Karen E. Seiger
Maps: altancicek.design, www.altancicek.de
Basic cartographical information from Openstreetmap,
© OpenStreetMap-Mitwirkende, ODbL
Printing und binding: Grafisches Centrum Cuno, Calbe
Printed in Germany 2024
First edition 2018
ISBN 978-3-7408-2399-3
Revised fifth edition, September 2024

Guidebooks for Locals & Experienced Travellers
Join us in uncovering new places around the world at
www.111places.com

Foreword

A year after college I moved to Washington to work at a historic hotel. It was there that I first heard stories from senior cooks, bellmen and waiters, some there since the 1940s, who had crossed paths with the powerful and famous. Many of the best tales I have ever heard are from the people behind the scenes of this storied city.

What I love most here are the changing seasonal colors. The cherry blossoms are the precursors to the kaleidoscopic bloom of spring. Cross-country skiers on Connecticut Avenue and community snowball fights on Dupont Circle brighten up winter. Nature's changes are accompanied by rotating highlights of the seasons in museums, theaters, restaurants, and gardens.

One of the greatest cultural benefits is the bounty of free museums, supported by taxes, members and benefactors, on and off the National Mall. The city has also been bestowed with many gifts to the country by other nations and spectacular private collections of art and historic artifacts.

The face of DC changes with every election cycle, as people come and go. The heart and soul of the city, though, lie in its heritage and diversity, colored by stories and feats of the generations before. We walk the same streets as the great thinkers who built this country, and the enslaved people who built our institutions with their hands. By its very nature the capital is cosmopolitan, home to people from around the world. The city is filled with tales of intrigue, peril, and conspiracy, of innovation, creativity, and generosity of spirit.

Enjoy the flavors and fragrances at a traditional Chinese tea house; sit under a true descendent of Newton's apple tree; explore a tiny fairy world at the foot of an old tree; and dance to Go-Go in a park dedicated to a hometown musical innovator.

DC is the seat of world power, but the city itself has a distinct funkiness, charm, and coolness. Come find your own stories.

– AMS

111 Places

1__50 States Bike Route

Cycle through every state in a single day

How can a person bike from Maine to California in a single day? The Washington Area Bicyclist Association (WABA) makes it easy each September with their annual 50 States Ride. The event takes 700 cyclists on a 62-mile (metric century, or 100 km) route that covers all the avenues that are named for the 50 states.

If you can't make it to the event, you can take the trip on your own any day of the year using the online maps posted on the Ride with GPS site after each year's ride. The routes vary somewhat from year to year, but the one thing that's certain is that they'll touch all 50 state-named avenues. If the 50 States Ride is a little too much of a commitment, see WABA's website for other fun rides. They've hosted the 13 Colonies Ride, a 15-mile (24 km) route along the avenues named for those states. They've done the 35-mile "Route 66," hitting eight avenues of the original states that the scenic highway passes through.

These rides are a wonderful way to see the sites throughout the capital. WABA's mission is to make biking enjoyable and safe in the Washington region (aka DMV). The routes are designed to take riders to areas that they might not normally visit, and also on a tour through US history.

You may see the magnificent Emancipation Memorial, also known as the Freedman's Memorial, in Lincoln Park as you ride along North Carolina Avenue SE. On Washington Avenue, SW, stop and pay your respects at the American Veterans Disabled for Life Memorial, honoring over 4 million veterans injured in the line of duty. On Louisiana Avenue NW is the Japanese American Memorial to Patriotism during World War II. The memorial's stunning bronze cranes tangled in barbed wire symbolize the internment of Japanese Americans in prison camps from 1942 to 1946.

Take in the diversity, history, and beauty. And enjoy a drink on the rooftop of the Yotel on New Jersey Avenue, NW.

Address Multiple points in Washington, DC; contact Washington Area Bicyclist Association: +1 (202) 518-0524, www.ridewithgps.com/events/187266-2022-50-states-ride, www.waba.org, events@waba.org | **Getting there** Search for "50 States Ride" on www.ridewithgps.com for current and prior-year maps | **Hours** Unrestricted | **Tip** For elegant handmade accessories, clothing, decor and chocolates, delicious food, and hard-to-find wines and spirits from Latin America, stop into La Cosecha at Union Market off Florida Avenue NE (1280 4th Street NE, Washington, DC 20002).

2__56 Signers Memorial
Chill out with the Founding Fathers

Constitution Gardens, including the Memorial to the 56 Signers of the Declaration of Independence, were dedicated for the US Bicentennial as a living homage to the founding of the republic. The memorial is nestled on a tiny island, reachable by wooden bridge. This mini oasis is a good spot to reflect on the actual people who risked livelihood, reputation, and even life to release the nascent country from the grips of King George III.

July 4, 1776 was the day the Declaration was adopted, not when voted on, nor when signed. The Committee of Five, Jefferson, Franklin, Adams, Sherman, and Livingston, were responsible for printing and circulating it to the 13 colonies. Overnight, 200 "Dunlap Broadsides" were printed in Philadelphia and dispatched on July 5. Only 26 originals remain intact today. The oldest signer, Benjamin Franklin, was 70, and the youngest, at 26, Edward Rutledge. Papers of the time were transported to different locations, and it appears that the writing in an unknown hand on the back of the Declaration was to identify it in a collection of rolled documents.

Hancock, of the conspicuous signature, was a smuggler of fine European goods. Sam Adams was a law school dropout. Franklin opened the first lending library. Jefferson was angry for life over the deletion of the anti-slavery paragraph. Gwinnett's signature is the most valuable to collectors. Harrison's son and great-grandson were later elected US Presidents. Rush published the first American chemistry book, and Hopkins co-built a telescope in 1769, used to track Venus' path. Whipple was a sea captain by age 21, and Lynch was lost at sea at 30. Witherspoon was the only college President, and Middleton a world traveler. Two brothers Lee signed.

After Pearl Harbor, the Declaration and Constitution were moved from the National Archives to Fort Knox, where they remained until war's end.

Address Constitution Avenue at 19th Street NW, Washington, DC 20245, www.nps.gov | Getting there Metro to Foggy Bottom–GWU (Blue, Orange, and Silver Line); bus 31, 32, 36 to Virginia Avenue & E Street NW | Hours Unrestricted | Tip The Lockkeeper's House is the oldest structure on the Mall, a tiny 1835 stone house where the lockkeeper collected tolls, tended the Washington City Canal locks, and raised 13 children (Constitution Avenue NW and 17th Street NW, Washington, DC 20006, www.nps.gov/nr/travel/wash/dc34.htm).

3 African American Civil War Museum

Telling the ancestors' stories Marquett, a young

African American Civil War re-enactor, dressed in a period infantry uniform, considers himself the face of the museum in that, by virtue of his stature, he represents "the average look, size, and age of a colored Civil War soldier." He and other staff members tell little-known stories of the formerly enslaved people and freedmen who had nothing to lose and everything to gain in their fight for freedom. Faces of men and women look out from the walls as if to call you over to read their stories.

This museum tells the oft-ignored history and contribution of the US Colored Troops (USCT), who were over 10 percent of Northern troops, in the war that ended slavery and preserved the union. The rich, complex, and difficult aspects of African American life before, during, and after the war are depicted not just in battle stories, but also in tales of community, survival, and the fight for freedom.

Tales of bravery and fearlessness abound. Child musicians, as young as eight years old, tapped out officers' commands on their drums in codes distinct for each regiment, to communicate with the mostly illiterate ranks. Troops knew the orders were for their regiment based on a drummer's introduction. Wilberforce University, a historically black college in Ohio, was shut down during the war, as so many students had enlisted in the 54th Massachusetts Regiment, the first USCT unit, as told in the movie, *Glory*. Two sons of abolitionist Frederick Douglass served, one in the Infantry and one in the Cavalry. President Lincoln ensured by June 1864 that all colored troops were paid equally, plus back pay, to their white counterparts.

On the first Saturday of each month, USCT descendants come to tell their ancestors' stories for the public and for the museum's archives. The museum is expanding into the adjacent building.

Address 1925 Vermont Avenue NW, Washington, DC 20001, +1 (202) 667-2667, www.afroamcivilwar.org | **Getting there** Metro to U Street/African-Amer Civil War Memorial/Cardozo (Yellow and Green Line); bus 90, 92, 96 to U Street and Vermont Avenue NW | **Hours** See website; outdoor exhibit unrestricted | **Tip** Directly across the street is the African American Civil War Memorial, "Dedicated to those who served in African American units of the Union Army in the Civil War." Former First Lady Michelle Obama's ancestors Jerry Suttor and Caesar Cohen, who served in the US Colored Troops, are there.

4 Albert Einstein Memorial

I myself should be dead already but I'm still here

One may walk or drive by and never notice Albert Einstein sitting quietly on semicircular steps. Albert is seated and holding a piece of paper with three of his most recognizable and important mathematical equations scribbled upon it: the Theory of General Relativity, the Photoelectric Effect, and the Equivalence of Energy and Matter. Einstein was selected as Time's "Person of the Century for the 20th Century," and his larger-than-life likeness now sits in an unassuming spot on the grounds of the National Academy of Sciences.

Don't for a moment think that he is just another pretty face in the landscape of sculpture and statues scattered all over the city. Walk up those few steps into his little garden and visit with the genius. Immediately notice what a perfect spot his lap and shoulders are for a memorable photo – visitors will want to snuggle up next to him and pose. Artist Robert Berks, known for his unique sculptural portraits, based this one on his 1953 study of Einstein in life.

There are three quotations inscribed on Einstein's bench that speak to his philosophical and humanitarian outlook towards the world. At his feet, there are over 2700 metal studs that represent the stars, sun, moon and other planets and celestial objects as mapped by astronomers on the memorial's dedication day of April 22, 1979, just weeks after the centennial of Einstein's birth.

But wait! There is an important secret within this monument to everyone's favorite theoretical physicist. Only one person can be standing on the statue at one time, including the surrounding steps, for it to work. Stand on the large dot representing the center of the planetary constellation at Albert's feet. Face the statue and speak directly to it, and you will hear your own voice in surround sound as it echoes off the statue. It feels like magic, but, as Albert knows, it's really science.

Address 2101 Constitution Avenue NW, Washington, DC 20418, on the grounds of the National Academy of Sciences, www.nasonline.org | Getting there Metro to Foggy Bottom–GWU (Blue, Orange, and Silver Line), walk south to Constitution Avenue NW; bus 42, 43 to Virginia Avenue & 19th Street NW | Hours Unrestricted | Tip Visit the five statues of Los Libertadores of Latin America: José de San Martín, Benito Juárez, Bernardo de Gálvez, General José Gervasio Artigas, and Simón Bolívar along Virginia Avenue NW, between 18th and 25th Streets NW.

5 American Geophysical Union Building

An architectural and engineering playground

The upgraded American Geophysical Union (AGU) headquarters is an ingeniously designed outpost for scientific collaborations and also a leading–edge model of Net Zero (using as much power as it generates over a year) and LEED (Leadership in Energy and Environmental Design) construction. It is the third-highest rated NetZero building in the US, paving the way for DC to become the greenest American city by 2032 by publicly sharing all of its data.

The AGU is anchored by the tenets of scientific discovery – innovation and action – which are imbued into the building itself. In the spirit of recycling and reusing, the compass rose as you enter is a remnant of the former lobby. The terrazzo floor and boardroom table are made of toilets, sinks, and urinals from the old bathrooms, crushed and blended into this pourable composite material. After some trial and error, to find the right combination of plants for the job, the hydroponic wall efficiently purifies outdoor air intake. Each floor carries a theme – Space, Atmosphere, Land, Oceans, Earth's Core – throughout the décor and images in the multiple conference rooms, where members can sit down together and collaborate on research and projects.

From the outside corner, the building resembles the bow of a ship. The brickwork reflects the density of the Earth's core layers, and the frieze identifies the disciplines of the AGU. Look down at the Solar System embedded in the sidewalk. It also serves as the hatch to the wet well and "core energy of the building," or gray water drawn from the city sewer system that provides much of its power and non-potable water.

At first glance, the AGU is a pretty building. For the curious, however, it is a playground of ingenuity, recycling, creativity in action, and the limitlessness of imagination and exploration. Every element of the building has a story. Go inside and take their free tour.

Address 2000 Florida Avenue NW, Washington, DC 20009, +1 (202) 462-6900, www.agu.org/building/pages/tour | Getting there Metro to Dupont Circle (Red Line), Q Street exit | Hours Exhibits: Mon – Fri 8:30am – 6pm; see website to schedule a tour | Tip A favorite hangout for embassy chefs, Bistrot du Coin's menu of French standards, including mussels and steak frites, hit the spot (1738 Connecticut Avenue NW, Washington, DC 20009, www.bistrotducoin.com).

6 Anacostia Park Roller Rink
This is how we roll

Unique to the National Capital Park system, the Anacostia Park skating pavilion is the only roller rink in the entire National Park Service. It is always free, but in summer it becomes a family and skate master's daily skate fest. From Memorial Day to Labor Day, the rink offers free roller skate rental of the old-fashioned 4-wheelers. Of course, you may lace up your own skates anytime throughout the year.

A rotating crew of DJs spins tunes every weekend evening in summer, which for the older set may be reminiscent of the roller rinks and moonlight skates of youth. DJ Graylin Presbury has been mixing sound at the rink since 1986, with crowd pleasing funk, oldies, R&B, go-go, rock, and top 40s. Off season, you have to bring your own beats. Serious DC skaters are known for their 360-degree jump spins, called snaps, and get their groove from their own headphones or from the DJs. Couples can often be seen "double" skating which looks like a flowing version of hand dancing on wheels. One partner, generally a lady, does most of the twisting and turning moves, with the hand of the other, a man, to provide the momentum for their energetic motion. Line dances may break out, while the veterans whiz around doing their signature moves or perfecting new ones, often at breakneck speed. For the novice or the rusty skater, the intimidation may feel real, but don't let it. If you ask, a veteran, or someone who's style you are grooving on, may just offer you some tips.

On a few weekends during the summer the Anacostia Rollers or other groups take over the rink for a synchronized performance that will leave onlookers clapping and cheering. The park itself was originally planned as a deep-water shipping lane and industry hub in the 1790s. Over a century, upstream agriculture caused silt build up, limiting viability as a port. Reclamation converted the swampy flats into a 1,200-acre park.

Address 1500 Anacostia Drive SE, Washington, DC 20020, +1 (202) 472-3884, www.nps.gov/anac/planyourvisit/roller-skating.htm | Getting there Metro to Potomac Avenue (Blue, Orange, and Silver Line) and walk across Sousa Bridge; bus U 2, V 7, V 9 to Pennsylvania Avenue and Fairlawn Drive SE | Hours See website for seasonal hours | Tip For a completely different trip around a rink, check out DC's roller derby scene. Members of the Women's Flat Track Derby Association, the DC Roller Derby, compete from February through August. Check their schedule at www.dcrollerderby.org.

7 Art-o-Mat

Art is a much better addiction

Those of a certain age will immediately recognize a neon-lit vintage cigarette vending machine labeled "ART*O*MAT," and then wonder what it is doing in the Luce Center at the Smithsonian. Come closer.

Insert $5 into the machine and pull a lever; out will drop a small box or cellophane-wrapped goody the size of a pack of cigarettes. Rip off the packaging to reveal your new, portable, wearable, or useable artwork. Just try and resist doing it again.

Though what exactly comes out is a crapshoot, you may select a category or an artist based on a tiny label above each knob or by peering into the machine to try to get a glimpse of what is within. The machine is filled with paintings, prints, fused glass jewelry, leather key rings, 3-D photocards, miniatures, and whatever else has been most recently added to the mix.

Clark Whittington, a North Carolina artist from the heart of tobacco country, was inspired to create the first Art-o-Mat when a friend had a Pavlovian response to the crinkling of a cellophane snack wrapper. The sound triggered in him the desire for a snack of his own, and the idea sprang to mind that the same response might inspire others to want to purchase actual works of art as well as candy. He refurbished an old vending machine and filled it with his own photographs mounted on wood blocks. He placed the machine in a local café and sold each piece for $1. So began what Whittington sees as "a way to encourage art consumption by combining the worlds of art and commerce in an innovative form." He hopes that his machine will create art collectors.

The Art-o-Mat in the Luce Center is custom built and can hold 176 pieces by 22 artists. Within the first 12 days after it was installed in 2010, art addicts consumed a collective average of 16 works of art a day. The truth is that pulling a knob on this vending machine just once is simply not enough.

Address Smithsonian American Art Museum, Luce Center, F and 8th Streets NW, Washington, DC 20004, +1 (202) 633-7970, www.artomat.org, americanartInfo@si.edu | Getting there Metro to Gallery Pl – Chinatown (Red, Yellow, and Green Line), or bus 80, P 6, X 2, X 9 to H and 9th Streets NW | Hours Sun – Sat 11:30am – 7pm | Tip Watch experts repairing and restoring art works from the collections of the three American art museums at the Lunder Conservation Center right down the hall.

8__Arts Walk

Art and poetry with beer

Arts Walk is a collection of over 25 studios at the Monroe Street Market, where local artists showcase and sell their work and offer classes, workshops, pop-up markets, and social gatherings. The joys of local artistry and craft abound here.

Black Lab features vibrant and stunning scarves, entrancing wall art, and handmade books, created from manipulated photographs by photographer Leda Black. Her Female Power Project graphics and accessories are bold and impactful.

Analog takes you back to the pleasures of non-electronic letter writing and materials. Think stationery, letterpress cards, journals, and more old school writers' delights. Vintage and reused materials and home goods are the essence of this studio.

The prints of original watercolors, mostly of food motifs and recipes, and illustrated cookbooks in Marcella Kriebel Art + Illustration are simply delicious. Kuzeh Pottery creates pieces in vibrant hues and shapely forms with a "touch of Persian spice." The pomegranate vases in an eye catching shade of red beg for a daisy or two, and the mugs with stylish handles simply must be added to one's morning coffee routine.

Tim Kime Art is a bonanza of colorful and joyfully upcycled furnishings and décor, where a fun conversation with Tim is always a delight. Studio 15 Artisans Domonique and Marcelle create vegan body products, repurposed African inspired train cases, nostalgic pillows of vintage pennants, and mini chicken art. The American Poetry Museum is the first museum solely dedicated to "collecting, interpreting, and presenting" the rich art form of American poetry, including spoken-word, through its literary programming.

Arts Walk hosts periodic themed art and maker festivals, such as Norooz and Earth Day, and a year-round Saturday farmers market. Take home an array of handmade items, plus fresh produce, coffee, breads, and other treats.

Address 716 Monroe Street NE, Washington, DC 20017, www.monroestreetmarket.com/
arts | Getting there Metro to Brookland-CUA (Red Line), then walk one block west on
Monroe Street NE; bus H 2, H 4, H 8, 80 and others to Brookland | Hours See website for
individual studio hours and events, most studios are open Thu – Sat | Tip The third Thursday
of every month from May to September is open studio night, when most studios are open
late and have snacks and drinks for visitors. A band plays on the stage on the plaza at the
end of the Walk, and Brookland Pint pours selected brews outdoors on the Walk.

9 Bald Eagle Nest
Mr. President and LOTUS among the azaleas

The US National Arboretum is one of the world's premier woody plant research facilities and public gardens, run by the US Department of Agriculture on 446 acres. Among its many horticultural collections are seasonal botanical and tree displays, tramways and trails, and even a grove of the original columns that supported the East Portico of the US Capitol building. While many flowers and shrubs within the arboretum bloom in the spring, there are attractions throughout the year, such as the Bonsai Museum, the National Grove of State Trees, the National Herb Garden, and the Asian Collection with its hardy camellias that bloom in late autumn. One standout among the arboretum's garden displays is the Azalea Collection. Every spring, thousands of azaleas cover the sides of Mount Hamilton and Glenn Dale Hillside in a blanket of color. The best way to see this spectacle is on foot via a network of rustic woodland trails.

In 2014, a pair of bald eagles, named Mr. President and First Lady of the US, or FLOTUS, raised their young atop a tulip poplar tree amidst the Azalea Collection – until FLOTUS flew away in 2019. Luckily, a new female eagle soon swooped in and captured Mr. President's heart. She was named Lady of the United States, or LOTUS, and they began a new family. Mr. President is quite the dad, but sometimes he has to be nudged out of the nest to do his fatherly duties as a hunter. Each season an online contest is conducted to name the new eaglets.

Volunteers from the American Eagle Foundation and the USDA maintain an eagle cam so the public can observe their activities without unwanted intrusion. But if you are lucky and persistent, you might see the eagles or hear their cries as they go about their daily lives as you walk along the paths near their tree.

So, when you visit the arboretum in spring or late fall, bring binoculars and be sure to cast your gaze both down to the flora and up into the treetops of this amazing natural environment.

Address 3501 New York Avenue NE, Washington, DC 20002, +1 (202) 245-2726, www.usna.usda.gov | **Getting there** Metro to Stadium Armory (Blue, Orange, and Silver Line) and transfer to bus B2 to Bladensburg Road at Rand Place NE, walk east on R Street NE to entrance | **Hours** Daily 8am–5pm, except Dec 25 | **Tip** Every year, the Arboretum hosts scientific and crafty workshops; special events and exhibits, such as the spectacular spring Ikebana exhibit; Full Moon hikes and children's activities. The seasonal bonsai displays in the National Bonsai and Penjing Museum are not to be missed at any time of the year.

10 Bartholdi Fountain
The fountain cousin of the Statue of Liberty

The centerpiece of elegant Bartholdi Park, part of the US Botanic Garden, is this allegorical Fountain of Light and Water. Frédéric Auguste Bartholdi, who later designed the Statue of Liberty, created it for the US Centennial Exposition of 1876 in Philadelphia, where it was placed at the center of the esplanade. The artist loaned it with the plan to sell it and more of the same design after the fair. At the time, Frederick Law Olmsted, the father of landscape architecture, was working on his commission to design the US Capitol grounds, and after the Expo, he urged Congress to buy the fountain. Bartholdi was paid $6,000 – half the asking price. In 1877, it was placed in the heart of the Botanic Garden on the National Mall, quickly becoming a favorite nocturnal destination, as it was one of the few places in the city that was lit up at night with gas lamps. The McMillan Plan of 1904 called for the beautification of the city and redesigning the Mall, so when the new Conservatory was completed in 1932, the gardens and fountain were moved to their current locations.

The 30-foot-tall fountain, made of iron cast in Paris at the storied Durenne Foundry, is painted to look like patinated bronze and weighs over 15 tons. Three sea nymphs, with headdresses of leaves and tiptoeing on shells and coral, appear to support a large crown of light. Water flows past joyful tritons and the nymphs above with robust fish and wide-mouthed turtles spouting water below. It is now lit by energy-efficient replicas of the original gas lamps.

The surrounding park is an educational and demonstration showcase of innovative plant combinations, edibles and natives, design trends, and gardening methods.

At twilight the fountain silhouettes against the setting sun for glorious photos. Once the sun goes down, and the lights come on, this becomes quite a lovely and romantic spot.

Address 100 First Street SW, Washington, DC 20534, +1 (202) 225-8333, www.usbg.gov/bartholdi-fountain | Getting there Metro to Federal Center SW (Blue, Orange, and Silver Line); bus 32, 36 to Independence Avenue and First Street SW | Hours Unrestricted | Tip The annual Poinsettia Exhibit is one of the highlights of the winter holiday season at the US Botanic Garden, the oldest, busiest public garden in the US, established by an act of Congress in 1820 (100 Maryland Avenue SW, Washington, DC 20001, www.usbg.gov).

11 Bathyscaphe Trieste
Dive to the deepest part of the ocean

Having invented a lighter-than-air balloon to ascend beyond the stratosphere, Swiss inventor Auguste Piccard then switched focus to the depths of the oceans. Only three men have reached the deepest part of the Challenger Deep at the bottom of the Marianas Trench. Two of them got there in Piccard's Bathyscaphe Trieste.

Piccard applied his theories of buoyancy learned in balloon flight to the Trieste, a navigable titanium diving vessel, with an observation gondola of 5-inch-thick steel, weighing over 14 tons. Its ballast was a mixture of heptane, water, and 9 tons of iron pellets in tanks that allowed it to sink. Ballast was released to control buoyancy and to allow it to resurface. It was completed in 1953 and named for the city of Trieste in Italy, where it was built. The Navy bought the vessel in 1956 and upgraded the pressure sphere in 1959 to withstand pressure up to 36,000 feet.

US Navy Lt. Don Walsh volunteered to go on the expedition to Challenger Deep, but a second volunteer would not step forth. So Piccard recruited his son, oceanographer Jacques Piccard, to take the second seat.

On January 23, 1960 Trieste descended for 4.75 hours to 35,814 feet. Exploration only lasted 20 minutes, as a Plexiglas window had cracked on descent, causing the vessel to shudder. They observed a brown "diatomaceous ooze" and deep-water flounder and sole, unexpected vertebrates to find at that depth. There was no publicity until they returned, as Admiral Arleigh Burke wanted no embarrassments if they failed. Journalists sniffed out the story but agreed with the Navy not to publish until after the mission.

Trieste was replaced in 1963 with Trieste II and moved to the US Navy Museum. The dents from the pressure of the sea are visible in the ballast tanks. The third explorer to reach Challenger Deep was James Cameron in 2012, though only to 35,787 feet. The museum is under renovation. Check the website for updates and online events.

Address US Navy Museum, Washington Navy Yard, 736 Sicard Street SE, Washington, DC 20003, +1 (202) 685-0589, www.history.navy.mil | **Getting there** Metro to Navy Yard-Ballpark (Green Line), walk east on M Street SE to 11th Street SE, turn right to Visitor Gate; bus 90, 92, P 6, V 5 to 11th and O Streets SE; ID or passport required | **Hours** See website for visitor access information | **Tip** Also in the museum, see scale models of early Naval ships, a captured Kamikaze training aircraft, and a model of Alvin, the submersible that helped locate RMS Titanic. Take a walk around the Navy Yard, the oldest continuously operating Naval base in the world.

12 — The Big Chair

A neighborhood symbol

In 1959, Bassett Furniture was commissioned to build a giant 19.5-foot-tall African mahogany chair, taller than the height of Lincoln seated in his monument and all major statues in DC, to attract shoppers to Curtis Brothers Furniture Company. At the time, it was the largest chair in the world and weighed over 2 tons.

The summer of 1960 brought the concept of "Alice in the Looking Glass House," an installation on the seat of the chair of a well-appointed 10' x 10' glass efficiency apartment, adorned with a tiny balcony and equipped with a full bathroom (hidden by a screen). A young woman named Lynn Arnold, the reigning "Miss Get Out The Vote 1960," was recruited by store employees in search of an inhabitant of the tiny apartment, as she shopped in the store, and moved into the apartment with the aid of a forklift for a 42-day "people staring" adventure. It was touted as an opportunity to "see her sleep, eat, exercise, and sunbathe, a sight you'll remember for years to come." Lynn received visits and phone calls from her husband and baby son and had her meals and fresh clothing sent up to her via a modest dumbwaiter.

During the riots of 1968 following the assassination of Dr. Martin Luther King Jr., this beloved sculpture was spared from the rampant destruction that was happening throughout the city, with the aid of armed sentries posted around it, as locals recall.

Over the years, the Big Chair has gone from being the motif of a store to a seat for Santa Claus and the Easter Bunny, to a destination for elementary school field trips. Many DC residents will recall a visit to Santa in the Big Chair as the highlight of the holidays of their childhoods. The wooden chair eventually weakened and was replaced by a $40,000 steel replica and continues to be a destination for school kids and visitors and remains a symbol of its Anacostia neighborhood.

Address Martin Luther King Jr Highway at V Street SE, Washington, DC 20020 | **Getting there** Metro to Anacostia (Green Line), turn left on MLK Boulevard and walk 4 blocks to the intersection of V Street SE | **Hours** Unrestricted | **Tip** Anacostia is changing every day, so a walk around the neighborhood might lead you to a different new spot from one month to the next. The neighbors love Mama's Pizza Kitchen where everything is fresh and "cooked with love" (2028 Martin Luther King Jr Avenue SE, Washington, DC 20020, www.mamaskitchenmenu.com).

13__Black Cat

Alt music and family tradition

Traditionally, Peaches O'Dell and her Orchestra ring in each new year at the Black Cat. On any other day, though, this place is seriously rocking out.

Two generations of Dante Ferrando's family were restaurant and club owners before him, and the original Black Cat was a pre-Prohibition restaurant and piano bar in New York. For over 25 years, Dante has been an innovator and a stalwart of the DC music scene. A punk rocker at heart, he was playing in three punk bands, Grey Matter, Ignition, and Iron Cross, when he decided to open the Black Cat in 1993. It has evolved into what he calls "a rock club with an arty bend."

As the music business shifts, Dante persists in bringing both legendary and up-and-coming local bands to his stages. Radiohead, Elastica, Corn, and Sugar Ray all played gigs here before they broke out. Indie and alt-rock are the mainstays, but it isn't unlikely to hear other beats or to have a specialty night to break up the constant flow of music. The uniqueness of his brand, unusual in the club scene, is the variety of music, art, and uncommon events that keep this venue vibrant in an ever changing music scene.

Belly up to the bar and enjoy a conversation with Lauren, bartender, traveler, and a proponent of the belief that music is a conversation starter.

Black Cat likes to show that things can be done distinctively. "Some aspects of the club are different than any other club because they can be!" Some elements harken back to other eras, like random seating, chalkboard menus, pool table, video games, and pinball machines. His underlying ethos is to create a venue where patrons want to hang out and where bands want to keep returning to play. He runs it like a "grassroots favorite" place, steeped in hospitality, colorful conversation, do-it-yourself décor, and a good beer list. The venue recently underwent a renovation, including moving the popular Red Room upstairs.

Address 1811 14th Street NW, Washington, DC 20009, +1 (202) 667-4490, www.blackcatdc.com | Getting there Metro to U Street/African-Amer Civil War Memorial/Cardozo (Green and Yellow Line); bus 52, 54 to 14th and S Streets NW or bus 90, 96 to U and 14th Streets NW | Hours Club hours vary depending on show times | Tip The Watermelon House was a happy accident. When the red paint job that the owners wanted didn't quite turn out to their specifications, they decided to make it into a showstopper. It looks like a house-size hunk of watermelon, seeds and all (1112 Q Street NW, Washington, DC 20009).

14 Bladensburg Dueling Grounds

Where gentlemen killed each other

Dueling originates in the tradition of single combat, where two sides pick a representative each, and they would fight to the death. In Europe, dueling became popular in the 16th century, particularly in France, where 10,000 men are said to have died in a single decade. The first duel in America took place at Plymouth Rock in 1621.

In 19th-century America, gentlemen settled their differences by dueling with pistols such as the large caliber smoothbore flintlock. Duels had all the trappings that we associate with them today – pistols at dawn, seconds, ten paces, and last-minute reconciliations.

Although dueling was illegal in the District of Columbia, that did not prevent them. It just required a small change of venue.

Just over the district line in Colmar Manor, Maryland, next to Fort Lincoln Cemetery, is the Bladensburg Dueling Grounds. Over 50 duels were fought on a small patch of grass from 1808 until the Civil War, including several after the Anti-Dueling Act was passed by Congress in 1839.

The most infamous of these duels was that between Stephen Decatur, hero of the Barbary Wars, and Joseph Barron. Both were US Navy Commodores, whose long-running feud began in 1806 when Barron made unflattering remarks about Decatur's personal life. The following year, at Barron's court martial for failure to defend his flagship, Decatur was one of the judges who voted to suspend him and then he took control of Barron's ship. In 1820, the two finally had their duel. Both were wounded, but Barron survived whereas Decatur died several hours later.

One end of the Dueling Grounds has a commemorative signpost of "The Dark and Bloody Grounds," and a bridge over Dueling Creek, from which you can see the entire park and imagine the scenes of gentlemanly conflict.

DUELING GROUNDS

On this site, now part of Anacostia River Park, more than 50 duels were fought during the first half of the 19th century. Here, on what became known as "the dark and bloody grounds," gentlemen of Washington settled their political and personal differences. One of the most famous disputes was that between Commodores STEPHEN DECATUR and JAMES BARRON, which was settled here on March 22, 1820. Commodore Decatur, who had gained fame as the conqueror of the Barbary pirates, was fatally wounded by his antagonist. Although Congress passed an anti-dueling law in 1839, duels continued here until just before the Civil War.

THE MARYLAND-NATIONAL CAPITAL PARK
AND
PLANNING COMMISSION

Address 38th Avenue at Bladensburg Road, Colmar Manor, MD 20722 | Getting there Metro to Rhode Island Avenue (Red Line) and transfer to bus B 9 to Bladensburg Road and 38th Street | Hours Unrestricted | Tip A few blocks west is DC Brau, the first brewery in DC since the demise of Heurich Brewing Company in 1956. Order up a Continuing Resolution 12 IPA or a Corruption IPA (3178-B Bladensburg Road NE, Washington, DC 20018, www.dcbrau.com).

15 __ Booth's Derringer

Assassination at the theater

The general facts surrounding the assassination of President Abraham Lincoln are well known. On April 14, 1865, the President and Mary Todd Lincoln were watching the play *Our American Cousin* in the Presidential Box at Ford's Theater. Actor and Southern sympathizer John Wilkes Booth entered the box and shot Lincoln at close range in the back of the head. Booth jumped down on to the stage, yelled "Sic semper tyrannis! The South is avenged," and ran out of the theater. The President died the following morning.

Booth was hunted down, shot by Union troops, and died three days later.

Ironically, Booth's older brother Edwin had been credited the previous year with saving Lincoln's son Robert from accidental death on a train platform.

To this day, one small artifact can be seen in the Ford's Theater Museum underneath where the fatal shot was fired. It is Booth's weapon itself, a small, one-shot .44 caliber Derringer pistol, easily concealed. So nobody would have guessed Booth's intentions that evening, and given the absence of a guard at the entrance, it was easy for the well-known actor to steal into the Presidential box to commit the heinous crime.

The pistol was designed by Henry Derringer and produced from 1852 until 1868. It was sold in pairs, not unlike the dueling pistols he had produced previously, in order to offset the limitation of a single shot by providing users with a backup second bullet. Booth's gun had the percussion firing system, a short barrel, a scrolled flourish and the "Derringer Philadelphia" mark typical of these pistols.

The gun's single shot design reflected Booth's determination to "do or die," and his actions reflected the opinion that Lincoln was a tyrant for his "War of Northern Aggression." The gun was seized by the government as evidence in the trial of Booth's co-conspirators. It was returned to Ford's Theater in 1940.

Address 511 10th Street NW, Washington, DC 20004, +1 (202) 347-4833, www.fords.org |
Getting there Metro to Metro Center (Blue, Orange, Red, and Silver Line) or Gallery
Pl–Chinatown (Green, Red, and Yellow Line); bus D6 to E and 10th Streets NW | Hours
Daily 9am–5pm; see website for tours | Tip Mary Surratt was one of John Wilkes Booth's
co-conspirators in the assassination of President Lincoln. The conspirators regularly met at
Surratt's home, which she operated as a boarding house, a few blocks away at 604 H Street
NW. A historic marker is mounted on the wall of what is now Wok and Roll restaurant.

16 Boundary Stone NW6

One of the oldest boundary markers of city limits

Under the mandate of George Washington, surveyor Andrew Ellicott and astronomer Benjamin Banneker, one of the first known African American scientists and the man who salvaged L'Enfant's city plan from memory, set out in April 1791 to survey and lay out the boundaries of the Territory of Columbia. Located at the convergence of the Potomac River and the Eastern Branch (now the Anacostia), it was selected by Washington for its strategic location between northern and southern colonies on an active shipping lane.

Banneker began at Point Lookout, Virginia, where he lay in a field for several nights and plotted 6 stars as they crossed a specific point at a specific time of the night. It was an astronomically selected spot where the cornerstone was laid with great ceremony by the men of Masonic Lodge 22, of which Washington was a member.

The surveying team broke a 40-foot-wide swath, 20 feet on either side of the border, each 10 miles long to form the boundaries of the city, carved from Virginia and Maryland. At each mile marker, a stone was set with magnetic compass coordinates on one side, the year of placement, "Jurisdiction of United States" on the DC side and "Maryland" or "Virginia" on the opposite side. On the northwest border with Maryland, the distance from stone NW4, the first in what remains DC, is also indicated on each stone. The Virginia portion of the city was retroceded in 1846. Of the 40 stones, 36 remain visible.

On Western Avenue at the intersection of Fessenden Street NW, is stone NW6, which is in poor condition, but easily accessible and surrounded by a gate and a historic marker. Two miles further south, off of Norton Street and the Capital Crescent bike trail is stone NW4, the oldest stone in the District. It is located inside the Dalecarlia Water treatment facility, best viewed from the fence line about 100 yards from the trail.

ORIGINAL FEDERAL BOUNDARY STONE
DISTRICT OF COLUMBIA
PLACED · 1791 · 1792
PROTECTED BY INDEPENDENCE BELL CHAPTER
DAUGHTERS OF THE AMERICAN REVOLUTION
1916

Address Boundary Park Neighborhood Conservation Area, 4700 block of Western Avenue at the intersection of Fessenden Street NW, Washington, DC 20015, www.boundarystones.org | **Getting there** Metro to Friendship Heights (Red Line); bus N4, N6 to Western Avenue and Fessenden Street NW | **Hours** Unrestricted | **Tip** In winter, head up Fessenden Street NW to Fort Reno, the highest point in the city, to join the neighborhood children and the young at heart on the great sledding hill on the west side of the fort. In summer, check out the weekend concerts and jam sessions on the East side of the fort (Chesapeake and 40th Streets NW, Washington, DC 20016).

17 ___ The Canterbury Pulpit

Martin Luther King's last sermon

The last Sunday sermon that the Reverend Dr. Martin Luther King, Jr. ever gave was on March 31, 1968 from the historic Canterbury Pulpit in the National Cathedral, the sixth largest Gothic Cathedral in the world. His sermon, "Remaining Awake Through a Great Revolution," spoke of a triple revolution of technology, weaponry, and human rights and urged the people to be alert and active in a time of great change and turmoil. The Nobel Peace Prize Laureate stood that day a marked man, only four days prior to his assassination in Memphis, Tennessee.

He spoke to a predominantly white crowd of over 4,000 people, that spilled out of the church into the yard, including many children who have grown up to become notable Washingtonians. He also declared that day that he planned to bring over 3,000 people to DC the next month for a non-violent demonstration. Instead, a memorial service was held at the Cathedral the following week.

Dr. King in the pulpit is immortalized with a stone carving in the north arcade, right above a visitor's head, as a tribute to his impactful presence that day. The facial expression and hand gestures give the carving life and makes his rich, syncopated baritone voice nearly audible.

The Canterbury Pulpit, from which Dr. King spoke, has a rich history of its own. The stone was a gift from the Canterbury Cathedral, once a part of the Bell Harry Tower, carved in England and presented to the National Cathedral in 1906, a year before the foundation stone was laid. It was not installed until 1929. Each person depicted in the carvings had a part in translating the bible from Latin into English. At the center is the Archbishop of Canterbury handing King John the Magna Carta to sign. The detailed scrollwork is a testament to the skills and dedication of the stone carvers who created this grand focal point for this national house of prayer.

Address Washington National Cathedral, 3101 Wisconsin Avenue NW, Washington, DC 20016, +1 (202) 537-6200, www.cathedral.org, communications@cathedral.org | **Getting there** Metro to Tenleytown-AU (Red Line) and walk or transfer to southbound bus; bus 31, 33 to Wisconsin and Cathedral Avenues NW or bus N 2, N 4, N 6 from Dupont Circle to Massachusetts and Wisconsin Avenues NW | **Hours** See website for hours and tours | **Tip** In the back of the Great Choir, on the arm of the second bench on the left is a carving of a lion eating a snake with the face of Hitler, symbolizing the Allies vanquishing the Axis.

18___Capital Pool Checkers
Crown Me!

As the former president of the Capital Pool Checkers Association, known by his Checker name (all members have one) "The Razor," puts it, this is the cheapest entertainment in town. This genial and competitive group convenes regularly to play pool checkers, which he notes is played similarly to bridge, canasta, and chess.

The association was loosely formed sometime during World War II. In 1982, it took hold in a local barbershop, but it got too big and disruptive, so it was moved to its long time home in Shaw and then recently relocated here. It is a place for people to get together over commonalities and competition to play a game that is favored around the world. Some 10 to 15 members win their way to the national championship each year. The strategies of pool checkers are not the quick and aggressive moves of the game of youth, but rather more deliberate, as in chess, though pieces are moved in different patterns.

Checkers is much older than chess, traceable to Iraq as far back as 3000 BC. A variation called Alquerque from 1400 BC was found in Egypt. Homer and Plato referenced checkers in their writing. A 12th-century Frenchman is credited with inventing Fierges, or Ferses, played on a chess board, which eventually found its way, presumably via maritime and trade routes, to England and the rest of Europe, and eventually to other continents.

On a regular basis in the evenings, a group of elder gentlemen and youth get together to play and compete, to exercise their minds, and socialize. A typical series is 14 games. Their tiny space in the heart of the Adams Morgan neighborhood invokes the feeling of a back-yard clubhouse. The small outdoor sign and unusual black-and-white mural of checkers players are enticing invitations to step inside. The club also offers periodic activities around the city.

While the association is a club of regulars, visiting players are always welcome. Come to learn or bring your best game.

Address 1750 Columbia Road NW, Washington, DC 20009, www.capitalcheckers.com,
capitalcheckers@gmail.com | **Getting there** Metro to Woodley Park-National Zoo (Red
Line); bus 42, 43 to Columbia Road and Ontario Road NW | **Hours** Sat evenings, hours
may vary | | **Tip** Visit Urban Dwell for fun and unusual gifts, including DC themed goodies,
a children's section, and a wall of crazy socks (1837 Columbia Road NW, Washington,
DC 20009, www.urbandwelldc.com).

19   Capital Slave Pens
Twelve years a slave in the cradle of freedom

Imagine going to a tavern for a pint of beer while you wait for the slave auction to begin. Or renting a basement room near the White House to keep your newly purchased slaves before taking them south to do your bidding. Or being chained together in a coffle, a string of men and women, and paraded past the US Capitol, which was built by enslaved people, on your way to be sold. All these scenarios happened regularly within sight of the three government branches established by the Declaration of Independence, which also states, "All men are created equal."

Abolitionists petitioned Congress in 1835–36 to end slavery in DC. They published a broadside calling Washington, "The Slave Market of America." Others called it "The National Shame."

William H. Williams owned the Yellow House and kept enslaved people in the basement, awaiting sale at auction. Robey's Slave Pen and Tavern was nearby, along with at least five others. The banks of the Potomac River were just down from the slave pens, prior to the addition of landfill to increase the southwest side of the city. Ships would dock, and enslaved people were either offloaded for sale in the pens and central market, or boarded to be transported to the South. Violinist Solomon Northrup, a freedman with papers to prove it, had come with two nefarious men to Washington from New York in 1841, thinking that he was going to perform with a circus. The two men took Northrup to a tavern and got him drunk. When he awoke, he was chained to the floor of the Yellow House. The men had collected their payment and left him to his fate. Later, he wrote of his experience in *Twelve Years a Slave*. Today, a marker tells of the slave trade here, and the approximate locations of the slave pens.

A provision in The Great Compromise ended slavery in Washington in 1850. In 1862, the DC Compensated Emancipation Act freed some 3,000 enslaved people and compensated former owners.

Address Independence Avenue at 7th Street SW, Washington, DC 20591 | Getting there Metro to L'Enfant Plaza (Blue, Green, Orange, Silver, and Yellow Line), Maryland Avenue exit; bus 74 to 7th Street and Independence Avenue SW or bus 32, 36 to Independence Avenue and 6th Street SW | Hours Unrestricted | Tip Look for as many as 40 species of butterflies in the Pollinator Garden (adjacent to the National Museum of Natural History, 9th Street between Madison Drive and Constitution Avenue NW, www.gardens.si.edu/our-gardens/pollinator-garden.html).

20__ Caruso Florist
Not just any flower shop

On any given day, Phil Caruso, third–generation co-owner of Caruso Florist, arrives around 5am at one of the oldest family-owned businesses in DC. After receiving flowers and orders, and making arrangements, he then holds court at the entrance for the last bit of his shift, greeting and chatting with customers.

Phil's grandparents, recent arrivals from Italy, began Caruso Florist in 1903 with a basket and a pushcart in Penn Quarter. After a long run in Columbia Heights, where their shop was destroyed by fire during the 1968 riots, they moved again and have been here in the heart of downtown ever since. The ice box in the back is 100+ years old, a relic salvaged from former quarters. Today, fourth generation brothers Michael and Stephen run the business alongside Phil and long-standing employees, one of whom was pirated thirty years ago from a local coffee shop.

Grandfather Joe used to walk the aisles of local wholesale houses, seeking out the best deals. Now, fresh flowers arrive daily from 30 to 40 countries and 6 continents. Back in the day, the family and their team would pull all-nighters making Mother's Day and Easter corsages. More recently, Michael's best friend, a DC Fire chief, recruited a large crew of off-duty firefighters to help deliver one enormous Valentine's Day bounty. Caruso has delivered 800 roses on a day's notice, decorated elaborate Indian weddings, made thousands of centerpieces, catered to a parade of regular customers, and arranged a flowered suitcase for a gypsy's safe passage from this life to the beyond. Michael and Phil have many stories to tell.

"Men mostly know roses, and women come in looking for colors and specific flowers," observes Michael. "You never know what you will get when the phone rings, or who is going to walk in the door, and that is what makes this fun." For the flower aficionado, it is a joy to stop in, say hello, and select some flowers from all over the world to brighten your own day.

Address 1717 M Street NW, Washington, DC 20036, +1 (202) 223–3816, www.carusoflorist.net, info@carusoflorist.net | Getting there Metro to Farragut North (Red Line) | Hours Mon–Sat 6am–5pm, Sun 7am–2pm | Tip For over 40 years, sisters and prolific authors Frances and Ginger Park have been selling fine chocolates from around the world and their own books at Chocolate Chocolate – "So good we had to say it twice!" (1130 Connecticut Avenue NW, Washington, DC 20036, www.chocolatedc.com).

21 Cedar Hill
Frederick Douglass had the best views

"What to the Slave is the 4th of July?" asked Frederick Douglass in 1852. Douglass, once enslaved, was a great American abolitionist, suffragist, reformer, orator, author, and statesman, among his many talents. He posed this question at a meeting of abolitionists in Rochester, New York eleven years before President Lincoln issued the Emancipation Proclamation. Indeed, independence for the United States meant very little to the African Americans who remained enslaved.

In 1877, Douglass purchased Cedar Hill, his final home, in present day Anacostia for $6,700 from the Freedmen's Savings and Trust Company with his first wife, Anna Murray. Anna too was an abolitionist and was a Station Master on the Underground Railroad. They enjoyed spectacular views of Washington, DC from their 8-acre hilltop home. Anna passed away in 1882, and in 1884, Douglass married Helen Pitts, an American suffragist and abolitionist who had lived next door to Cedar Hill and who happened to be white.

Helen inherited Cedar Hill upon Douglass' death in 1895 and dedicated the rest of her life to establishing their home the Frederick Douglass Memorial and Historic Association. She preserved his legacy for us to appreciate and continue to learn from today. You can still see many of the original furnishings and personal objects. The library is particularly wonderful, with its bookshelves filled with over 1,000 volumes. His sturdy roll top desk and chair look as though he just stepped away. See if you can spot his top hat.

The house can only be visited on a 30-minute tour guided by a National Park Service ranger. Rangers impart insightful personal stories from the Douglass archives and details of his home life, work, and legacy that is still felt today. The bookstore is filled with Douglass' own writings and many other books and items related to African-American history.

Address 1411 W Street SE, Washington, DC 20020, +1 (202) 426-5961, www.nps.gov/
frdo | Getting there Metro to Anacostia (Green Line); bus B 2, V 2 to W and 14th Streets
SE or bus 90, P 6 to Martin Luther King Jr. Avenue and W Street SE | Hours See website
for hours | Tip The Anacostia Community Museum is the smallest of the 20 Smithsonian
museums. It is a model of creativity in developing exhibits that speak to Washington, DC's
history and diversity (1901 Fort Place SE, Washington, DC 20020, www.anacostia.si.edu).

22 Ching Ching Cha

Taking tea in the Chinese tradition

Ching Ching gracefully pours hot water over tea leaves in a cup or pot used expressly for the type selected. She allows it to sit for a few moments while explaining the ritual of the flavor palate to attentive patrons. The infusion is discarded into a bowl on the table, and fresh water poured over the seasoned leaves, now open, to steep.

After 25 years in Georgetown, the teahouse moved to a beautiful new location in Dupont Circle with a renewed concept that includes tea service and shopping for dozens of curated types and flavors of loose-leaf tea interspersed with cookbooks and children's books. Peruse the rotating selection of Asian market bags, adornments, home goods, and elegant canisters to store tea properly. All styles of teapots, mugs, cups, infusers, and small gifts decorate the inviting retail space. Staff can assist in the selection of the proper serving vessel. Petite pots and cups for Oolongs and Pu-erhs; clear glass for jasmine and flowering teas and small clay pots for green, white and black teas. Chinese tea service, practiced here, is an art.

Ching Ching explains, "We have a certain expectation when we have tea. We want it hot and in small servings. Having water on the table is very important to keep tea hot and fresh." All her teas are sourced directly from small farmers in China, Taiwan, and Japan. When she began this odyssey, she spent months learning tea customs in Taiwan and had the honor of sitting with an all-male group of Tea Masters in Japan for the offering of the first tea of the season. The first tea picked is placed in a jar and offered to the Buddha in an elaborate, traditional ceremony.

After so many years in business, she has many regular customers. She laughs, "Sometimes I feel like a doctor because people always ask about the health benefits of teas." She elaborates on the greens and the Pu-erhs and exclaims, "I get so excited over the Oolong shipment at the first of the season!"

Address 1314 21st Street NW, Washington, DC 20036, +1 (202) 333-8288, www.chingchingcha.com, tea@chingchingcha.com | Getting there Metro to Dupont Circle, exit at Connecticut Avenue & 19th Street NW, walk south on 19th Street NW, west on N Street NW, and north on 21st Street NW | Hours See website | Tip The Kreeger Museum is a private modern art museum showcasing works by Kandinsky, Monet, Noguchi and other in the former Mid-Century Modern home of collectors David & Carmen Kreeger (2401 Foxhall Road NW, Washington, DC 20007, www.kreegermuseum.org).

23__Chuck Brown Park

A shrine to the Godfather of Go-Go

Going to a dance party when Chuck Brown headlined was a spectacle. The inventor and "Godfather" of Go-Go music always put on a rocking marathon of a show and holds a warm place in the hearts of music lovers.

Go-Go, a syncopated rhythm of percussion and bass, has its roots in funk, soul, blues, and salsa in the 1960s. The term 'go-go' first referred to places where young people were partying and then became the name of the DC-grown music genre. The percussion section never stops playing, and the bandleader involves the audience in an animated call and response between songs, which also serves as a shout out for announcements in the house. A blogger said, "If you listen carefully…you'll hear the heartbeat and humanity of a very proud DC community."

Situated a few blocks off the Rhode Island Avenue corridor, Chuck Brown Park is a hip tribute to this much loved beacon of DC spirit and artistry. In the shape of a guitar pick, surrounded by flowering trees that bloom a lively purple and pink in spring, the park welcomes visitors with the sound of children playing. Chuck is embodied in a brightly colored, slatted sculpture by Jackie Braitman. It is strips of cascading metal that change depending on where you stand: a guitar from some perspectives, and from head-on, it is a colorful figure of the Godfather himself, one hand holding his guitar, the other outstretched holding a microphone, as if reaching out to amplify the voices of his audience.

There are toy drums and chimes for children of all ages to play. Along the back of what doubles as a stage is his discography engraved on aluminum panels, and a tiled, photorealistic mosaic chronology of his life in show posters, photos, and quotes. Chuck looms large and almost pops off the memorial wall: smile, dark glasses, gleaming teeth, and black hat trademarking his memorable look, style, and energy.

Address 2901 20th Street NE, Washington, DC 20018 | Getting there Metro to Rhode Island Avenue (Red Line), transfer to bus B 8 Fort Lincoln or 83 Cherry Hill to Rhode Island Avenue and 20th Street NE, walk 2 blocks south to the park | Hours Unrestricted | Tip Chuck Brown Day is the annual Go-Go dance party held in mid-August, generally on the third Saturday, with several bands commemorating Chuck Brown's music and legacy. See website for location. (www.windmeupchuck.com).

24__Colonel Dahlgren's Leg
Buried with full military honors

Around knee height on Building 28, a plaque marks the approximate location of the original tomb of the leg of Civil War Colonel Ulric Dahlgren, son of Admiral John Dahlgren, father of American Naval Ordnance. In July 1863, Dahlgren was shot in the foot during a skirmish with Confederates in Hagerstown, Maryland, and a few days later the leg had to be amputated. In the heat of summer, there was no time to return his leg to Philadelphia for burial in the family gravesite, so the decision was made to entomb it in the wall of the foundry that his father was building at the Navy Yard to produce artillery for the war effort. Enclosed in a lead-lined wooden box, the leg was interred within the Victorian industrial foundry's cornerstone with full military funeral, including an honor guard.

Dahlgren recuperated and returned to service with a wooden leg, riding on horseback with his crutch tied to the saddle. But he was killed eight months later in a failed Union raid on Richmond, Virginia. Orders to capture or kill Jefferson Davis, President of the Confederacy, were found in his pocket by a 13-year-old looter, who gave them to his teacher. The body was unceremoniously buried among Confederate soldiers but was shortly after exhumed under dark of night with the aid of three gravediggers, paid $1,500 (over $33,000 today) cash. Dahlgren, sans a finger cut off to steal a ring, was temporarily reburied on a Unionist's land and ultimately returned to the family plot. The "Dahlgren Papers" were circulated widely, and it is presumed that their existence inflamed the conspiracy to assassinate President Lincoln.

The foundry was demolished and replaced in 1915, then again in 1942, and the cornerstone remained – but the leg did not. In 1998, the second building was demolished for a parking garage. The plaque was recovered. The mystery of the leg remains.

Address Washington Navy Yard, Building 28, Isaac Hull Avenue SE (near Tingey Street SE), Washington, DC 20003 | Getting there Metro to Navy Yard-Ballpark (Green Line), walk east on M Street SE to 11th Street SE, turn right to Visitor Gate; bus 90, 92, P6 to 11th and O Streets SE; ID or passport required | Hours See website for visitor access information | Tip While on base, have a Guinness in honor of Colonel Dahlgren (and his leg) in Mordecai Booth's Public House, whose hours encourage day drinking (1411 Parsons Avenue SE, Building 101, Washington, DC 20003, www.navymwrwashington.com).

25 — Crypt of James Smithson

Laid to rest in his legacy

Today, the Smithsonian Institution is the world's largest museum complex, comprising 19 museums and the National Zoo. But did you know that it owes its origins to a foreigner who never once set foot in the United States?

James Smithson was the illegitimate son of the 1st Duke of Northumberland who became a mineralogist and chemist, and for whom the mineral Smithsonite is named. His will directed that his fortune be given to his nephew, Henry James Dickinson, but it also stipulated that, "In the case of the death of my said Nephew without leaving a child or children, or the death of the child or children he may have had under the age of twenty-one years or intestate, I then bequeath the whole of my property… to the United States of America, to found at Washington, under the name of the Smithsonian Institution, an Establishment for the increase and diffusion of knowledge among men."

James Smithson died in 1829, and his nephew died six years later without heirs. The US Congress accepted the Smithson bequest in 1836, but it wasn't until 1846 that the Smithsonian Institution was founded. Work on the main Smithsonian Institution building, a Romanesque Gothic work called The Castle, was completed in 1855.

Meanwhile, Smithson had been buried in Genoa, Italy. By the early 20th century, the cemetery was making way for a quarry, so Alexander Graham Bell accompanied Smithson's remains to Washington, DC. He had finally made it to America! Smithson's remains were entombed on the first floor of The Castle, which is undergoing a major renovation.

The monument itself has extensive symbolism. An urn is supported on lions' feet representing strength. Carvings of moths represent life after death, laurels for victory, birds for ascension, serpents for wisdom, a scallop shell for rebirth, and a pinecone finial for regeneration.

Address Smithsonian Castle, 1000 Jefferson Drive SW, Washington, DC 20560, +1 (202) 633-1000, www.si.edu/Exhibitions/smithson-Crypt-796 | **Getting there** Metro to Smithsonian (Blue, Orange, and Silver Line); bus 52 to Independence Avenue and 12th Street SW | **Hours** Unrestricted from the outside due to renovations; enjoy a virtual tour of the interior at naturalhistory2.si.edu/VT3/castle/z_castle-001.html | **Tip** On either side of the World War II Memorial is the familiar face of a long-nosed man with big hands, peaking over a wall, with the words "Kilroy was here" etched into the stone (1964 Independence Avenue SW, Washington, DC 20227).

26__Culture House DC

Abandoned church becomes an art centerpiece

Once an active church built in 1886, Friendship Baptist fell into disrepair, and was nearly lost to urban blight. It was reclaimed in 2012 by the SW Arts Club and Blind Whino partners and converted into an experiential art and event space. The evolution into a neighborhood staple was a bit of a happy accident, as the founders were still formulating their vision as the collective evolved.

Public artist HENSE, whose "process and product is a unique battle between the beauty of fine art and the bricolage of the street," refaced the outside in bright sweeping abstracts that beckon a viewer on the street to come closer. Upon entering, the eye meets a visual smorgasbord of colors and patterns. Every wall is covered by murals, ornate and intricate, realistic and straightforward, and created by artists from the area and around the world. The downstairs rotating gallery is changed regularly, featuring local and regional artists, a specific theme, or visitor-created, interactive wall art.

The stage of the upstairs auditorium, flanked on both sides by regal, roaring lions that seemingly leap from the walls, is the focal point for music, dance, and other performances. Vintage stained-glass windows, embossed metal ceilings, and colorful painted walls can be enjoyed from the former choir loft.

Culture House DC is growing its reach into the arts community, partnering with local art collectors, smaller theaters, dance companies, and event organizers to bring diversity of art into the neighborhood. It will soon anchor an art district that is currently in development by the owners of the Rubell Family Collection. With every visit, a new perspective prevails.

Unusual small festivals, ebullient music shows, dance performances, and art exhibits can be found on Culture House DC's event calendar. You can also rent this cool venue to hold your own event.

Address 700 Delaware Avenue SW, Washington, DC 20024, +1 (202) 554-0103, www.culturehousedc.org, info@culturehousedc.org | Getting there Metro to Southwest Waterfront (Green Line); bus P6 to M Street at Delaware Avenue SW or bus 74, A9, W9 to M Street at 4th Street SW | Hours Sat 11am–2pm; see website for events and exhibitions. | Tip The newest museum in the city, Rubell Museum DC, a family-owned collection originated in Miami, showcases and elevates some of the most compelling new artists of the day (65 I Street SW, Washington, DC 20565, www.rubellmuseum.org).

27__Da Vinci's de' Benci
She flew in a first-class window seat

A $53 American Tourister, hard-sided, dark gray, 3-suiter suitcase, "outfitted like a thermos jug" to maintain the temperature and humidity, transported Ginevra de' Benci's portrait from the palace vault in Liechtenstein to the National Gallery of Art in 1967. She had just been purchased for $5 million ($36.7 million today), the highest price ever paid in the art world, and flew strapped safely into a window seat in first class alongside her handler with unseen, elaborate security precautions.

In 1960, the Director of the National Gallery visited the museum of the Princes of Lichtenstein with a curator, who led him through a trap door into a sub-basement wine cellar where the greatest treasures were stored. Here, he came upon the 1474 portrait of the lovely Florentine aristocrat Ginevra de' Benci, hanging from a nail.

The portrait appears to have been sold around 1605 when her family, the second wealthiest behind the Medicis, died out, and was later sold in 1733 to the Princely Family of Liechtenstein. It was hidden from the Nazis in a monastery and then smuggled into Vaduz Castle during World War II. After years of flirtation with her owners, the day came when the monarchy was in deep debt, and Prince Franz Josef II agreed to sell the portrait to the young gallery, which had gained global standing after hosting the Mona Lisa, loaned by President Charles de Gaulle to President John Kennedy, for half a million visitors to see.

Likely commissioned for her engagement at age 16, as her rightward facing countenance indicates, Ginevra is the only Leonardo da Vinci painting in the Americas. It is an innovative work in that he painted her in a natural setting, rather than indoors, using the new medium of oil paint, with brushstrokes to indicate he had yet to control it, and in his sfumato style.

The best photo is of the telescoping rooms that frame her as you look into her gallery.

Address National Gallery of Art, 6th Street and Constitution Avenue NW, Washington, DC 20565, +1 (202) 737-4215, www.nga.gov | **Getting there** Metro to Judiciary Square (Red Line), or Archives-Navy Memorial-Penn Quarter (Yellow and Green Line); bus 32, 36 to Pennsylvania Avenue and 7th Street NW | **Hours** Daily 10am–5pm | **Tip** The Canadian Embassy Art Gallery showcases the diversity of the art, culture, and nature of our neighbors to the north (501 Pennsylvania Avenue NW, Washington, DC 20001, www.connect2canada.com/art-gallery).

28 Dance Place

This is dance central

Dance Place, often referred to as "the hub of dance activity in Washington," is coming up on 50 years as one of the anchors of the local arts scene.

Formed in 1978 by Carla Perlo and Steve Bloom as a dance and school outreach program, it was gentrified out of its previous space and moved to a permanent home in a modified warehouse in Brookland, at the time a quiet residential neighborhood adjacent to Catholic University and the National Basilica. Dance Place is now firmly planted as the pillar of culture within the community.

The 144-seat theater hosts over 100 performances per year in a diverse range of styles. World dance, particularly West African, has a special place in the repertoire, and a collection of partner dance companies perform here regularly. Dance festivals and celebrations of culture and holidays are held each year to bring a variety of movement and sound to the stage, such as tap, African, hip-hop, and modern dance. One notable favorite of tap dance festivals is Baakari Wilder, the Assistant Artistic Director of Capitol Tap.

The hamlet that Dance Place has built up is now an arts campus that has been integral to the development of this ever-more animated neighborhood. Dance classes are available for all ages in a number of disciplines. Their community garden is used for after-school educational programming, and summer arts camps for children to engage body and mind. The plaza between the main stage and the rehearsal rooms is the perfect spot for free outdoor community music and fitness programs intended to engage neighbors, visitors, and passersby in artful and social ways, and whenever there is a Brookland-wide festivity or a citywide arts event, Dance Place is involved.

The shows are exciting and the audiences are extremely enthusiastic. There is a contagion of happiness and talent here that you must experience for yourself.

Address 3225 8th Street NE, Washington, DC 20017, +1 (202) 269-1600, www.danceplace.org, ideas@danceplace.org | **Getting there** Metro to Brookland–CUA (Red Line); bus 80, G 8, H 2, H 4 to Monroe and 7th Streets NE | **Hours** See website for class and event schedule | **Tip** Just down the street, the Dew Drop Inn is a great spot to hang with the neighbors for a cold beer, either inside amidst vintage ephemera or outside adjacent to *Out of This World*, the fun mural by Tim Kime (2801 8th Street NE, Washington, DC 20017, www.dewdropinndc.com).

29 DC Fire and EMS Museum

City history through a firefighter's lens

At the side entrance of the historic DCFD Engine Co. 3 station, a retired lieutenant enthusiastically greets visitors at the door, leads them through the active station, and heads up in the tiny elevator to the museum. The door opens to a sizeable wood-paneled room filled with a large collection of well-arranged red, yellow, and black artifacts made of brass, metal, and wood: DC firefighting history dating back over 130 years.

An 1804 law required that buildings have a fire bucket on every floor for bucket brigades to pass water along to extinguish a fire, like the one you can see from the home of Philip Barton Key, son of Francis Scott Key. Call boxes, like the one that looks like a lamp, were found on street corners from 1873 to 1949 to sound a fire alarm. Firefighter badges collected from every state and DC are pinned on a US map. A wonderful photo collage of the entire DC Fire Department of 1903 sits beneath a 20th-century alarm mechanism.

Ticker tapes from a 1929 4-alarm fire at call box 157, which is code for the White House, and a thank you note from President Hoover are some remnants of a fire that burned the West Wing during a Christmas Eve staff party. It began either with an overheated electrical wire or a stopped up chimney and a pile of old pamphlets stored in the attic above. Three hours, 135 men, and over 20 trucks later, the executive offices were in rubble.

The working life of a fire horse was not more than six years. With every fire alarm, a three-horse team would get hooked up to a four-ton steamer engine and run through the streets to the fire. The last such engine, No. 18, used from 1905 to 1921, is parked alongside the modern fire trucks downstairs. It is with great pride and storytelling skill that the volunteers at this museum share the history of a service that has preserved and sustained a city since the 1790s.

Address 439 New Jersey Avenue NW, Washington, DC 20005, +1 (202) 673-1709, www.friendshipfireassoc.org/home/fire-museum | Getting there Metro to Union Station (Red Line); bus D6 to E Street and New Jersey Avenue NW | Hours Send email to ships00@aol.com for tour reservations | Tip The National Fire Dog Monument, "Ashes to Answers," a tribute to the invaluable contribution of arson dogs, is located down the street at Engine Company #2 (500 5th Street NW, Washington, DC 20001, arsondog.org/nfdm-about).

30 __ Department of the Interior Murals

Painting our American lives

Inside the Department of the Interior (DOI) building, called "a symbol of a new day" when built after the Great Depression, is a trove of 40 murals commissioned to keep artists working, and to beautify the space in the spirit of the agencies operating within. One percent of the building's cost, or $127,000, was allocated to acquire art in 1935. Harold Ickes, the first and longest serving Secretary of the Interior, oversaw every element of construction and filled it with more art than any other federal building. Today, half a percent of the budget is still used to buy and preserve artwork. Some of the finest artists of the 1930s painted these walls: Maynard Dixon, Allan Houser, Gifford Beal, John Steuart Curry, Stephen Mopope, William Groper, and James Auchiah. Three themes are evident: Native Americans, resource reclamation, and the work of DOI agencies.

Throughout the building, Indians, homesteaders, pioneers, scenes from the Dust Bowl and New Deal industrialization are illustrated.

In an old ice cream parlor, black-and-white floors are complemented by frescoes on every wall in vibrant indigenous hues of sky blue, earthen red and verdant green.

Gerald Nailor depicts his Navajo subjects in soft shades with rounded features. Potawatomie Woodrow Crumbo's *Wild Horses* and *Buffalo Hunt* echo the wild motion of animals on the run. Allan Houser shows Apache life and rituals. Velino Herrera's triptych of Pueblo life beautifully shows in one scene the intricate pottery designs for which his tribe is well known. Downstairs, frescoes by Kiowa painters Stephen Mopope and James Auchiah adorn the pediments of the employee cafeteria. Though some of the motifs may look similar, the distinctive and striking styles remind us of the rich American landscape that is our national heritage.

Address 1849 C Street NW, Washington, DC 20240, +1 (202) 208-4743, www.doi.gov/
interiormuseum/Tours | Getting there Metro to Farragut West (Blue, Orange, and Silver Line)
or Farragut North (Red Line); bus 32, 33, 36 to H and 18th Streets NW | Hours By tour only
Tue & Thu 2pm, reservations required | Tip Since 1938, the DOI's Indian Craft Shop has been
buying directly from Native American artists nationwide. Shop for jewelry, pottery, carvings,
and sculpture by artists from nearly 60 tribes. Don't miss the rich book section.

31 Dupont Circle Fountain
Hangin' with the Rear Admiral

In the late 19th and early 20th centuries, the Dupont Circle neighborhood was the hub for high society as evidenced by the splendid mansions. Residents included Sissy Patterson, heiress to the Washington Post, and Alice Roosevelt Longworth, daughter of Theodore. Later in the century, Dupont Circle evolved into a well-established gay neighborhood, hosting colorful clubs, bookstores, and shops, and was affectionately known over the years as Fruit Loop. With age, it has mellowed.

In 1871, the Corps of Engineers began construction of Dupont Circle, which at the time was called Pacific Circle. In 1882, Congress authorized a memorial statue of Rear Admiral Samuel Francis du Pont in recognition of his Civil War service. Du Pont is known for capturing San Diego during the Mexican-American War, the establishment of the US Naval Academy, his victory at Port Royal and his early successes maintaining Civil War military blockades, and his controversial attack on Charleston, South Carolina in 1863.

In 1921, the statue of Du Pont was replaced by a tiered white marble fountain that stands there to this day. The du Pont family did not care for the statue and felt that a fountain was an appropriate tribute to a Navy man. It was designed by sculptor Daniel Chester French and architect Henry Bacon, the man responsible for the Lincoln Memorial. Three classical figures symbolizing the Sea, the Stars, and the Wind are carved on the fountain's central shaft along with a dolphin and other maritime figures.

At any time of the day or night, the circle bustles around the fountain with serious pick-up chess matches, bike couriers, and remarkable people watching. On most weekends, the New Orleans Jazz Band will jam for hours. The Circle is alive with movement, conversation, and music. Whether you're sitting on a bench or passing through, time spent there will be thoroughly entertaining.

Address Intersection of Connecticut, Massachusetts, and New Hampshire Avenues NW, Washington, DC 20036 | Getting there Metro to Dupont Circle (Red Line); bus 42, D 2, D 6, G2, L 2, N 2, N 4 to the vicinity of Dupont Circle | Hours Unrestricted | Tip One of the last bastions of the old-school gay establishments is The Fireplace where peanut dispensers are remnants of the days when nuts were the only edibles served here. The long-time bartenders and customers have great stories to tell (2161 P Street NW, Washington, DC 20037, www.facebook.com/thefireplacedc).

32 Dupont Underground

From tracks to treasure

Once a forlorn, abandoned trolley station, Dupont Underground is now a captivating subterranean public space showcasing a vast array of inventive art forms from tagging (graffiti for the non-urban) to video to theater and music.

In its original form, it was built as the storage facility for inter-urban trolleys in use from 1949 through 1962, when the trolley system was shut down. From that time until 1974, during the Cold War, the tunnels were outfitted to be a fallout shelter to accommodate 1,400 people with two weeks of provisions. It was dormant until 1995 when it reopened as a short-lived food court, whose developer ended up in jail for scamming his investors. Again, the space was known only in the memories of long-term locals and squatters.

In 2016, after years of rediscovery, renegotiation and renovation, the first phase of Dupont Underground opened with *Raise/Raze*, in which plastic balls from a National Building Museum project were reimagined into a Lego style build-your-own-and-tear-it-down architectural installation. Contemporary and street art is elevated here, from kaleidoscopic, pulsing tags to photography, to electronic installations, and periodically rotating exhibits. Plan on visiting Dupont Underground more than once because the next time you stop by, you may just see a brand new work of art.

Located below the bustling Dupont Circle, with its entrance at hip height right across from the Hotel Dupont Circle, it is best visited with walking shoes. The original tiled walls, street exit signs, vaulted spaces, and trolley tracks remain as a nod to its former life, and will be fully incorporated into the future development of the site.

Currently open periodically for evening tours, exhibits, special events, and maker markets. It is intended over the next several years to become a 75,000-square-foot multi-use urban art, retail, and business destination.

Address 19 Dupont Circle NW, Washington, DC 20036, www.dupontunderground.org, connect@dupontunderground.org | **Getting there** Metro to Dupont Circle (Red Line); bus 42 to Connecticut Avenue and Q Street NW, or bus L 2 to Connecticut Avenue and R Street NW | **Hours** See website for hours and events | **Tip** Fantom Comics is the store of choice of local comic book fans of all stripes. Known for its comic reservation service and unusual events, this shop is well worth a visit (2010 P Street NW, Washington, DC 20036, www.fantomcomics.com).

33 — Earliest Cherry Trees
They survived blight and keep on blooming

The National Cherry Blossoms that adorn the city in inimitably breathtaking fashion each spring are dear to Washingtonians.

Eliza Scidmore instigated the effort to bring cherry trees to Washington. On visits to Japan she fell in love with their blooms, and she proposed to officials that they would be a perfect addition to the city. Further inspired at a 1909 lecture by a USDA scientist who had determined that the DC climate would be ideal for them, especially along Speedway (now Independence Avenue), Scidmore set out to buy some. She wrote to First Lady Helen Taft, who joined the effort. A Japanese chemist heard about the campaign and proffered that Tokyo donate 2,000 trees. Mrs. Taft accepted, and the trees arrived in January 1910 – infested with nematodes, bugs, and disease! President Taft sadly had to have them burned, but some were saved. The Tokyo mayor offered a second shipment of 3,020 trees of 12 varieties. In February 1912 they arrived, dedicated in March by Mrs. Taft and Iwa Chinda, wife of the Japanese Ambassador to the US.

The oldest yoshino cherry trees seem to predate both gifts, planted in 1910 on Hains Point on fresh landfill just dredged from the Potomac River. Judging by the space between the trees, it appears that these 24 gnarly old dames were planted away from the National Mall in what may have been a quarantined section to see whether blighted trees could thrive. The spacing helped them avoid spreading insects and disease. Through DNA testing it is known that these trees are not the same as the 100 remaining from the 1912 shipment, and their origin is still nebulous. They are considered some of the most historic trees in the US.

The site of these centenarians in full bloom is stunning. As their gossamer, pale pink petals flutter in the breeze, they serve as a reminder that such a symbolic gift of peace between friends is also a gift of beauty.

Address East Potomac Golf Course, 972 Ohio Drive SW, Washington, DC 20024 | **Getting there** Metro to Smithsonian (Blue, Orange, and Silver Line), Independence Avenue exit, and walk about 1.4 miles; metro to Southwest Waterfront (Green Line), walk to The Wharf and take the free jitney across the channel (seasonal); Viewable up close by playing a round of golf. Otherwise, adjacent to the driving range. | **Hours** See website for seasonal hours | **Tip** The National Cherry Trees generally bloom in late March to early April. The Cherry Blossom Festival is a month-long event with festivities and exhibits throughout the city (www.nationalcherryblossomfestival.org).

34 Electronic Superhighway
Neon ode to the American road trip

Many stop for a few minutes to look at it. "Oh, look at that cool map!" Upon closer examination, one may note that the video looping within the different colored neon outlines of each state is reflective of the uniqueness of place, though some are rather obscure. Idaho potatoes, JFK in his motorcade, and classic movie clips of *Showboat*, *Oklahoma*, and *The Wizard of Oz* imply that much of what is conceived about the country is from movies and television. It can be a treasure hunt of state symbols.

Nam June Paik arrived in the US in 1964, shortly after the creation of the American superhighways. In the 1960s, Dinah Shore sang from our TVs, telling us to "See the USA in your Chevrolet," which inspired Paik and many a traveler. He conceived this kinetic map in 1995 – a tribute to the Great American Open Road and all of the grandeur and scenery that can be found along the way, even as one whizzes by in a car.

The Great Lakes and rivers flow in blues and greens, and one might even visualize the spot where Niagara Falls flows. The states are outlined in all colors, to show their individuality, even in the current age of information. The neon is meant to invoke the colors of flashing roadside motel and restaurant signs that both beckoned travelers onto the open highway and invited them to come in off the road for the evening.

After a recent gallery update, the map is now viewable in its full resplendence. Can you spot DC? There is a tiny old closed-circuit camera that isn't showing any discernible video until you look more closely and realize that it is your moving image in the DC camera.

Paik, considered the father of video art, coined the term "electronic superhighway" in 1974, with the idea that the world could be connected by technology. This work implies that we are so absorbed in electronic media, that it has perhaps replaced the physical discoveries of the great road trip.

Address Smithsonian American Art Museum, F and 8th Streets NW, Washington, DC 20004, +1 (202) 633-1000, www.americanart.si.edu | Getting there Metro to Gallery Place–Chinatown (Red, Yellow, and Green Line); bus 80, P 6, X 2 to H and 9th Streets NW | Hours Daily 11:30am–7pm | Tip In the window of the newly renovated Chinatown Express, ladies pull handmade noodles and make savory dumplings. Come in for lunch, dinner or an after-hours snack to try the fresh noodles or steamed pork buns (746 6th Street NW, Washington, DC 20001, www.chinatownexpressdc.com).

35 Evalyn Walsh McLean House

Where the Hope Diamond owner spent her teens

Balinese statues guard the entrance of this Gilded Age Beaux-Arts mansion, purchased for a song in 1951 as the Embassy of Indonesia. Evalyn Walsh McLean, a nouveau riche heiress of Irishman Tom Walsh, who struck it rich out west in the gold rush, lived here as a teen and inherited it in 1932. Her father moved his family to DC at the turn of the 20th century, when everyone with money was moving here and building lavish mansions. The house, built for $853,000 ($27 million today) boasts a carved Y-shaped staircase resembling that of a deluxe ocean liner, a custom Tiffany skylight, two ballrooms, early elevators and a massive organ.

Evalyn spent her teens in an environment of lavish parties, hosting royalty, socialites, diplomats and spies. She and her husband Ned McLean, owner of the Washington Post until 1933, moved up the road and continued the tradition of hosting extravagant, wild parties. Evalyn was plagued by alcohol and drugs, and lived with abandon.

As for the necklace… Imagine wearing a 45.52 carat blue diamond, the largest ever mined and cut, as everyday jewelry. Evalyn did just that. While the exact provenance of the diamond is not precisely known, it is presumed to have been cut from an original raw stone of 112 carats, sold by a diamond merchant in the 1660s to the Sun King of France, who had it cut into a 67-carat heart, which he dubbed "French Blue." It was passed down the line of monarchs, and after the French Revolution in 1792, it was smuggled out of France and into the collection of King George IV. In 1839, it was acquired by London banker and diamond collector Henry Phillip Hope. Given the size and description, even without provenance, it was concluded that the Hope Diamond could only have been cut from the French Blue. In 1911, Cartier brought it to DC and talked Evalyn into buying it for $180,000 ($5.3 million today).

Address Embassy of the Republic of Indonesia, 2020 Massachusetts Avenue NW, Washington, DC 20036, +1 (202)775-5200 | **Getting there** Metro to Dupont Circle (Red Line); bus N 2, N 4 to Massachusetts Avenue and 20th Street NW, or bus 42 to Connecticut Avenue and Q Street NW | **Hours** Mon–Fri 9am–5pm; tours by appointment only, information@embassyofindonesia.org | **Tip** To immerse yourself in a gorgeous, Gilded Age mansion, take a free tour of the Anderson House, home of the Society of the Cincinnati. They also offer regular public music, art and literary programs (2118 Massachusetts Avenue NW, Washington, DC 20008, www.societyofthecincinnati.org).

36 Exorcist Steps & Stories

Terrifying and head-spinningly steep

It's been over 40 years since people began calling the notoriously creepy Georgetown stairway the "Exorcist Steps." Known primarily for their frighteningly steep angle, the 75 stone steps, originally known as the Hitchcock Stairs, were built in 1895 alongside the Car Barn, which was a transit hub for four consolidated trolley lines serving DC and Virginia. The stairs were used for commuters to make transfers among trolley lines that ran out of 3 floors and the roof. Picture the ladies at the time, hoofing up and down 75 steps at a near right angle while wearing long dresses, petticoats, corsets, big hats, and pointy shoes! Athletes "running the steps" today have nothing on these women. Georgetown students soon discover that the stairs are a shortcut from Key Bridge to campus, and they have been running up and down them since 1895.

And then came *The Exorcist*, the 1973 horror movie that had people literally fainting in theaters. Novelist William Peter Blatty, a 1950 graduate of nearby Georgetown University, was inspired by a real-life story of a 1949 exorcism of a boy possessed in nearby Maryland, and also by this claustrophobic set of stairs from his college days.

Blatty and Director William Friedkin chose to use several sites on the Georgetown campus and the adjacent house at 3600 Prospect Street NW. They had to build a false front onto the house to make it feasible for the possessed character of Father Karras to catapult himself out the window and tumble to his death down the stone stairway. The stunt double earned his keep, throwing himself down the famous stairs twice during filming, with only a mere half-inch of padding on each step.

Now largely unknown to anyone who didn't see the movie in theaters or on a VCR, *The Exorcist* is still a very scary film. Watch it online and then go climb the stairs. At night. If you dare.

Address Prospect at 36th Street NW, Washington, DC 20007 | **Getting there** Bus 31, 33, or DC Circulator (Georgetown–Union Station Route) to Wisconsin Avenue and N Street NW | **Hours** Unrestricted | **Tip** The Tombs, rowing themed pub, is a favorite of the Georgetown University crowd. It was the model for the pub in *St Elmo's Fire* and used for a few scenes in *The Exorcist*. Named for a line from T. S. Eliot's poem, *Bustopher Jones: The Cat About Town*(1226 36th Street NW, Washington, DC 20007, www.tombs.com).

37__FDR Desk Memorial

A minor yet mighty presidential memorial

Franklin Delano Roosevelt was the President during tumultuous times in American history. Between 1932 and 1944, he led the government during the Great Depression and World War II, establishing firm allies in the process. In 1997, a large memorial to FDR located in West Potomac Park was dedicated by President Clinton. But there was already another, little-known memorial to him, and one that he would have preferred to the one established more than 50 years after his death.

At the southeast corner of 9th Street and Pennsylvania Avenue NW, on the grounds of the National Archives, sits a simple rectangular, white marble block. With the Archives behind it and the Navy Memorial across the street, it is easy to miss if you are not looking for it. On the block are engraved the words: "In Memory of Franklin Delano Roosevelt 1882 – 1945." The plaque next to it explains why it is there and why it more closely follows FDR's wishes for a modest memorial.

In 1941, FDR told his friend and Supreme Court Justice Felix Frankfurter, "If any memorial is erected to me, I know exactly what I should like it to be. I should like it to consist of a block about the size of this (putting his hand on his desk) and placed in the center of that green plot in front of the Archives Building. I don't care what it is made of, whether limestone or granite or whatnot, but I want it plain without any ornamentation, with the simple carving, 'In Memory of.'"

On the twentieth anniversary of his death, several family members and close friends dedicated the original memorial to FDR, made of marble from the same quarry that provided his gravestone in Hyde Park, New York. President Lyndon Johnson missed the dedication but later laid a wreath there. While the larger FDR memorial teaches about his accomplishments and honors his legacy, be sure to cross the National Mall to the memorial that he approved himself.

Address Corner of 9th Street NW and Pennsylvania Avenue NW, Washington, DC 20408 | Getting there Metro to Archives-Navy Memorial-Penn Quarter (Green and Yellow Line); bus 32, 36 to Pennsylvania Avenue and 7th Street NW | Hours Unrestricted | Tip The big stone head sitting in front of the National Museum of Natural History is an exact replica of the 5.84-foot San Lorenzo Colossal Head #4, one of the 17 known Olmec Colossal Heads from Veracruz in southern Mexico (10th Street NW and Constitution Avenue NW, Washington, DC 20560, www.naturalhistory.si.edu).

38 Fort Stevens
Civil War skirmish in the capital

But for the Battle of Harpers Ferry that engaged the Confederate Army for four days, which then paused near DC, and a sniper's shot missing the President by inches, the tide of the Civil War and history might have been significantly different. The Battle of Fort Stevens is lost to history as minor, but had the plans of generals on both sides gone to the advantage of the Confederacy, Washington, the grand prize, would have been taken.

President Lincoln and his generals noted the capital city's vulnerability after the Union Army's 1861 defeat at the first Battle of Manassas, 30 miles south. With that, the Army Corps of Engineers was tasked with building Washington's defenses – a ring of 68 forts, with every high point and depression protected every 800 to 1,000 yards, connected by roads, communication, and supply lines. By 1864, DC was the most fortified city in the world.

In July 1864, Confederate General Jubal Early was sent to strike what spies told was a poorly guarded capital, after General Grant had taken reinforcements to Richmond. Meanwhile, Major General Fry assembled 500 men able to ride a horse out to engage the enemy. Early moved into the area on July 11 with 14,000 troops and skirmished to test the line. The next day, he took aim at Fort Stevens, which had been reinforced overnight by Grant's troops.

President Lincoln fearlessly rode his carriage from his cottage nearby to visit the troops on July 12. He stood on the parapet of Fort Stevens to survey the situation, and a sharpshooter's bullet whizzed past him. A surgeon next to him was injured. A soldier shouted, "Get down, you damn fool!" Grudgingly, he stepped down at the behest of his Secretary of War, mumbling, "I thought I was the Commander in Chief." To date, he is the only President to come under enemy fire.

Early retreated that night after seeing how quickly the Union could rally its troops. Commemoration events are held annually.

Address 6001 13th Street NW, Washington, DC 20011, www.nps.gov/places/fort-stevens.htm | Getting there Bus 70 to Georgia Avenue and Quackenbos Street NW, or bus 52, 54, 59, E 4, S 2 to 14th Street and Missouri Avenue NW | Hours Unrestricted | Tip Battleground National Cemetery was dedicated by President Lincoln after the Battle of Fort Stevens. 41 of the fallen soldiers were buried here. The last burial was held in 1936 for 92-year-old Edward R. Campbell. Each July, on the Saturday closest to the 12th, the National Park Service commemorates the battle.

39 Franciscan Monastery

Catacombs, martyrs, and a mummified child

This spiritual oasis is a place to be stirred by nature, church, spirit, and art, and is home to some of the most lush and beautiful landscapes in the city. It was founded in 1898 to provide religious pilgrims the ability to visit the Holy Land without traveling abroad. The Holy Land Franciscans have for over 800 years been the guardians of the sacred treasures of Christianity. Here they are self-sufficient, generating much of their own food and water.

The Memorial Church is an amalgamation of architectural styles echoing the sacred structures of the Holy Land and Italy. It was designed by Italian architect Aristide Leonori, now on his way to sainthood for having built a church or basilica on every continent.

Above ground, the Altar of Calvary is an exact copy of the one on the crucifixion site in Jerusalem. One may follow in the steps of Christ and put oneself in the places where his life's milestones occurred, an unusual and fascinating opportunity for the faithful and others alike.

Descend beneath the Sacred Heart altar, following a vein of tufa limestone, through a passageway of trompe l'oeil crypts to the tombs and catacombs. Intricate mosaics in sepia shades line the Purgatory Chapel, made from images on oil paintings by women in an Italian village who specialized in the craft, whose work on them was delayed during World War II. Over the tomb of Saint Benignus, a martyred 2nd-century Roman general, is a Renaissance style sculpture originally of wax, which melted in its case and had to be sent back to Italy to be remade in stone. His bones are in a glass reliquary atop the pink marble tomb. Saint Innocent, a mummified child martyr of unknown name, lies in his ornate robes, the bones of his small hands visible.

Even friars get hazed. They are sent into the catacombs with the lights off, and they must find their way out so that they may stay in the order.

Address Franciscan Monastery of the Holy Land in America, 1400 Quincy Street NE, Washington, DC 20017, +1 (202) 526-6800, www.myfranciscan.org | **Getting there** Metro to Brookland–CUA (Red Line); bus H6 to 14th and Quincy Streets NE, or bus 80 to 12th and Quincy Streets NE | **Hours** Church: daily 9am–4pm, see website for church and catacomb guided tours; Gardens: daily 9am–4:45pm | **Tip** Take your thoughts into nature with a walk through Fort Bunker Hill, one of the remnants of the Civil War Defenses of Washington (14th & Perry Streets NE, Washington, DC 20017, www.nps.gov/places/fort-bunker-hill.htm).

40___Frank Kameny Gravesite

Gay rights pioneer is not buried here

While Washington's gay community was being decimated by AIDS in the 1980s and 1990s, Congressional Cemetery was one of the few willing to allow victims to be laid to rest there, as it was yet unclear whether the disease could still spread in death. It is here that HOBS, a non-profit gay rights group, bought a gravesite for Dr. Frank Kameny, the man considered "The Father of Gay Rights."

After a short professorship, Kameny, a PhD and World War II combat veteran, took a job as an astronomer at the Army Map Service. Shortly, reports of his sexuality triggered an investigation. He was fired in 1957 for being gay and in 1958 was barred forever from holding a federal job. After a series of congressional appeals, lawsuits, and an appeal to President Dwight D. Eisenhower, he failed to get his job back. He wrote a salient brief to the Supreme Court in 1961, yet they denied his case – twice. His is historic for being the first sexual orientation-based civil rights case ever taken to the highest court.

Kameny was a man of many firsts. He co-founded The Mattachine Society, the first gay rights organization, followed by the National Gay Rights Lobby. He was the first to lead protests at the White House, State Department, Pentagon, and Civil Service Commission, and the first homosexual to run for Congress. Though he did not win, he paved the way for others who have followed and won elections. He was instrumental in getting homosexuality declassified as mental illness by the American Psychiatric Association.

Kameny strived to show that his actions were about acceptance in the eyes of the law, rather than "gay power" and militancy. Kameny died at 86 on National Coming Out Day in 2011. His legal heir battled with HOBS over ownership of the grave. In the Gay section, the only one in the country, his military cenotaph indicates subtly that there are no remains beneath.

Address 1801 E Street SE, Washington, DC 20003, +1 (202) 543-0539, www.congressionalcemetery.org | Getting there Metro to Potomac Avenue (Blue, Orange, and Silver Line); bus 32, 36 to Pennsylvania Avenue and Potomac Avenue SE | Hours Daily dawn–dusk, may vary for funerals and events | Tip Stop by the home of George Cassiday, the official bootleger to Congress during Prohibition. He was so popular that lawmakers set him up with an office in the Capitol complex (303 17th Street SE, Washington, DC 20003).

41 Gallaudet University
The epicenter of the deaf world

Called the "epicenter of the deaf world," Gallaudet was the first college in the world for students who are deaf or hard of hearing. It shares a campus with schools where youth are educated from infancy to graduate school. The institution is a global leader in DeafSpace design, brain and language research, and education methodology. Students are bi-lingual in American Sign Language (ASL) and English, and foreign students are multi-lingual in their native sign and written languages, along with ASL and English.

A statue of Thomas Gallaudet and Alice Cogswell represents the man behind the institution and his young neighbor who sparked his life's passion for educating deaf children. On a research trip in Paris, Gallaudet met Laurent Clerc, a deaf educator who was teaching in a non-verbal, French communication system. They returned to the US in 1817 to found the country's first school for the deaf in Hartford, CT. Gallaudet's son Edward later moved the school to DC, renamed it for his father, and became its first president. In 1864, President Lincoln signed the bill into law that allowed the institution to confer college degrees. In 1986, the school was granted university status, and in 1988, the "Deaf President Now" movement resulted in its first deaf leader.

The campus is rich in traditions and stories, including a superstition that any student who passes through the coffin-shaped door in College Hall will not graduate. The football huddle was invented by the Gallaudet team so that opposing players could not figure out the plays being called. There is also an annual funeral for rats. Freshmen hold an elaborate service for a male and a female rat (once real, now toys), with a coffin full of class mementos, a formal burial, and a marker for the dearly departed rodents. Look for headstones all over campus. Learn more by visiting the Gallaudet University Museum, and scheduling an ASL/English guided tour of campus.

FRIEND
TEACHER
BENEFACTOR

THE DEAF PEOPLE OF THE UNITED STATES
IN GRATEFUL REMEMBRANCE OF
THOMAS HOPKINS GALLAUDET
MARK THE CENTENNIAL OF HIS BIRTH
WITH THIS MEMORIAL
1887

Address 800 Florida Avenue NE, Washington, DC 20002, +1 (202) 250-2474
(videophone) or +1 (202) 651-5050 (voice), www.gallaudet.edu/maguire-welcome-center,
visitors.center@gallaudet.edu | Getting there Metro to NoMa – Gallaudet U New York
Ave (Red Line); bus 90, 92 to Florida Avenue and 7th Street NE | Hours 9am – 5pm; see
website for daily tours in ASL with voice interpreters | Tip Layers upon layers of crunch
make the croissants at Pluma by Bluebird Bakery irresistible, not to mention the sweet
goodies like croissant monkey bread and flaky crusted pastries (391 Morse Street NE,
Washington, DC 20002, www.plumabybluebird.com).

42 __ Game Fish
Look at what we hooked!

The home of the Renwick Gallery of American Craft is the building originally designed by Architect James Renwick for the Corcoran Collection, the first building in the US built specifically as an art museum. The museum owns and exhibits works of craft, from rustic to that which borders on fine art. The line is often fine itself. Among its permanent collection are furniture of Sam Maloof; an Albert Paley gate; fine textiles; Gullah basketry; and eclectic jewelry. The grand staircase, with an orange carpet resembling spilled paint, is lit by an infinitely programmed chandelier by Leo Villareal.

One of the most eclectic works in the permanent collection is the showstopper, *Game Fish*, by Larry Fuente. At over four feet high and nine feet long, it looks like no sailfish you will ever encounter on a fishing trip.

Fuente is well known for transforming ordinary and found objects into unusual works. Among his renowned works is one of the greatest examples of the art car movement. He spent five years coating a 1960 Cadillac sedan, *Rad Cad*, with a million brightly colored beads, sequins, buttons, plastic lawn ornaments, and other trinkets. *Cowasaki*, is a motorcycle covered to appear like a steer. The horn sounds like a cow mooing and the tail is lifted to add gas via its backside.

Game Fish arrived at the Renwick in 1991. Constructed of epoxy, polyurethane resin, and plywood, it is covered with plastic baubles, buttons, and mass-produced items that make it the most fanciful sailfish imaginable. Take a good look at the dorsal fin to find dominoes, billiard balls, Disney characters, Superman, plastic combs, paint brushes, yo-yos, miniature gilded bowlers and bowling pins, toy cars and ships, doll heads, baby blocks, and even a Smurf. *Game Fish*'s arm – yes, it has one – holds a dart at the ready, as if its bead-covered elongated bill were inadequate.

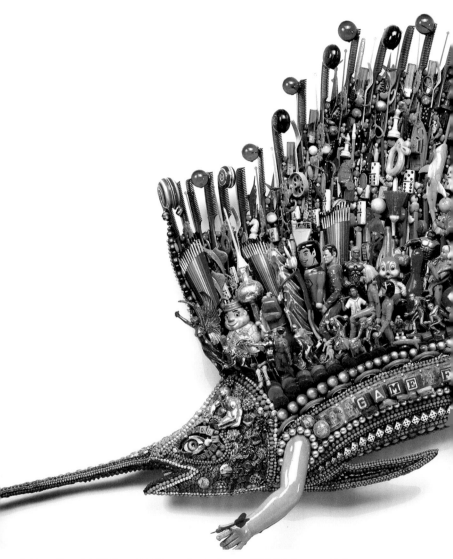

Address Renwick Gallery, 1661 Pennsylvania Avenue NW, Washington, DC 20006, +1 (202) 633-7970, americanart.si.edu/visit/Renwick, americanartinfo@si.edu | Getting there Metro to Farragut West (Blue, Orange, and Silver Line) or Farragut North (Red Line); bus 42 to 17th and I Streets NW | Hours Daily 10am–5:30pm, closed Dec 25; *Game Fish* is currently hanging in the gift shop. | Tip "Somewhere in an alley," for over 30 years, The Well-Dressed Burrito has been feeding tasty and bountiful portions of Tex-Mex favorites to people who work in the neighborhood. Order ahead for pick-up or walk in for weekday lunch only (1220 19th Street NW, Washington, DC 20036, www.thewelldressedburrito.com).

43__George Mason Memorial

A neglected Founding Father

George Mason is most remembered for authoring the Virginia Declaration of Rights as a delegate to the Constitutional Convention of 1787, and for withholding his signature, along with two others, from the US Constitution, as it neither abolished slavery nor provided adequate protection of individuals from the federal government. He is noted for having said, "I would sooner chop off my right hand than put it to the Constitution as it now stands."

Mason had the unique idea of the day that legally binding, inalienable individual rights were more important than government, which he thought was overzealous and ill-defined. His writing is echoed in Thomas Jefferson's words in the Declaration of Independence. He is considered the Father of the Bill of Rights, as his Virginia document provided the foundation from which James Madison wrote the Bill of Rights that was added in 1791 in the First Congress to allow the people to curtail the power of government and the judiciary. Slavery was not rescinded.

The contemplative seated statue of Mason was incorporated into the Pansy Garden, and in spring is lush with vibrant colored flowers. In winter, it is a stark and elegant figure, even more charming in the snow. The seated statue of Mason, a voracious reader, is accompanied by a stack of books, his tricorn hat, and cane. Inscriptions of some of his writings can be read on the wall behind him.

The placement of this memorial near the Jefferson Memorial is symbolic of the friendship between the two men and their mutual concerns for civil rights. The memorial was called one of the "finest pieces of public art" by a long-serving member of the Fine Arts Commission. Artist Wendy Ross said, "I chose to depict Mason shortly before his death in 1792, when he witnessed the culmination of his long quest to establish individual rights as a fundamental aspect of government."

Address Ohio and East Basin Drive SW, Washington, DC 20242, www.nps.gov/nama/planyourvisit/george-mason-memorial.htm | **Getting there** Metro to Smithsonian (Blue, Orange, and Silver Line), exit Independence Avenue SW, walk around Tidal Basin past Jefferson Memorial | **Hours** Unrestricted | **Tip** About halfway between the George Mason Memorial and Independence Avenue, along the riverside path, is a bolder with a brass plaque to commemorate the first air mail service that began from this field on May 15, 1918 between Washington and New York.

44 Georgetown Flea Market
Upscale picking

Every Sunday, the Georgetown Flea Market is aflutter with vendors from as far as Philadelphia selling their goods. Furniture, antique table linens, and decorative housewares are intermingled with ethnic imports and jewelry. This market was the 1972 brainchild of lawyer Mike Sussman.

Just inside the main gate, vintage jewels are beautifully arranged in large glass cases. Guilloche enamel, Taxco sterling, and gold filigree catch the eye. A West African artist sells bright, twisted copper wire jewelry made by her own hand. Baltimore John, always in the rear parking lot on 34th Street, has one of the best booths for picking. He sells mostly jewelry and small vintage items that he finds around the region. Poking through his boxes of intertwined chains, earrings, and brooches is a messy proposition, but the results of your efforts will be rewarded with goodies that conjure the days of digging through grandma's jewelry box. For the crafty shopper, his booth is often a goldmine of vintage chandelier crystals and bohemian beads.

One of the best bargains is for the bicycle owner. If you arrive early enough, Wayne from Virginia tunes up bikes on the spot in about 45 minutes. If repairs are substantial, he may take your bike to his shop and return it the following week. He travels with a selection of used bikes, and his service and prices are unbeatable.

Come early for the best selection and peaceful shopping. The place gets warmed up around 11am. For better deals, especially on a harsh weather day, bargaining may improve at the end of the day, though it varies by vendor. Some are firm on their pricing as "we do a lot of searching to bring these items to our customers, and no one makes a fortune selling in a flea market." And then there are those like John who may haggle a little more, especially if your hands are full or you are a regular.

Address 1819 35th Street NW, Washington, DC 20007, in the parking lot of
Hardy Middle School, main entrance at Wisconsin Avenue and 34th Street NW,
www.georgetownfleamarket.com | Getting there Bus 31, 33 to Wisconsin Avenue and
34th Street NW | Hours Sun 8am–4pm | Tip Georgetown Neighborhood Library's
Peabody Room hosts an extensive special collection of Georgetown artworks and
historical documents including home histories for nearly every house in the neighborhood,
and the Mapping Georgetown project (3260 R Street NW, Washington, DC 20007,
www.dclibrary.org/georgetown).

45 — Georgetown Labyrinth
Contemplation along the waterfront

At the northernmost navigable point on the Potomac River, efforts to create a national park over the course of 30 years resulted in the Friends of Georgetown Waterfront Park. It boasts biking and skating paths; a spray fountain and pergola; and one of only a few labyrinths in the District not on religious ground, located on the western end of the park. Labyrinths have a long history beginning with Greek mythology. An elaborate structure was built by Daedalus for King Minos of Crete to hold the Minotaur. Depictions of single course labyrinths became popular in coinage as early as 430 BC.

Although labyrinths became synonymous with the mazes that became popular starting with the Renaissance, they have only one entrance and path that winds through a circle, while mazes have multiple entrances and dead ends. The curving turns of the labyrinth are meant to encourage contemplation as the traveler walks from the outer edge into the center and back out again. The number of quadrants and circuits varies in meaning and context.

In religious settings, the labyrinth may represent the long and arduous path to God, the pursuit of enlightenment, or a symbolic pilgrimage to the Holy Land. To some Native American tribes, they are the representation of Mother Earth. In some cultures' pagan rituals they are used as the setting to pay homage to goddesses, and in Scandinavia, where trolls and wild winds reside, they serve as ocean-side traps to prevent these impudent forces from impeding good fishing.

The intent of this labyrinth is to "foster spirituality and connection among people of all cultures" in this bright, undulating park. Clear your head. Walk slowly, focus on quieting your mind and disconnect from the chaos of the outside world. Walk purposefully and peacefully, and take in the views of the river and the skyline to realign your spirit.

Address 3303 Water Street NW, Washington, DC 20007, +1 (202) 895-6000, www.nps.gov/places/georgetown-waterfront-park.htm | Getting there Metro to Foggy Bottom–GWU (Blue, Orange, and Silver Line); bus 31, 33, 38B to M Street and Wisconsin Avenue NW | Hours Daily dawn–dusk | Tip Dog Tag Bakery makes delicious baked goods and great sandwiches, served in a bright and cozy shop on a side street. All proceeds are used to provide education, training and job skills to disabled veterans and their caregivers (3206 Grace Street NW, Washington, DC 20007, www.dogtagbakery.com).

46 __ Gorby Intersection

Gorbachev stops traffic and thaws the Cold War

On a December day in 1987, Mikhail Gorbachev, in town for a summit with President Reagan, stopped his motorcade in the middle of the lunch rush hour on Connecticut Avenue NW to the amazement and thrill of everyone around. His heavy, black vehicle screeched to a halt, and he and Vice President Bush, who was riding with him to the White House, got out of his car. It took a few moments for the lead security vehicle and the lunchtime crowd to figure out what was going on. The lead car backed up and the crowd closed in.

The Secret Service and KGB officers became frantic as Gorbachev walked around shaking hands, saying hello, and waving to shocked Washingtonians. A translator accompanied him to speak to people nearby. Officers were yelling into their radios, "He's out of the car! He's shaking hands!" And to the crowd, "Keep your hands out of your pockets!" And, in Russian, probably something similar. Two blocks over at the Russian Embassy on 16th Street, the message came over a security radio, "We have a traffic problem at Connecticut and L."

The commotion got the attention of people inside office buildings, who opened their windows and started waving at the spectacle. On the balcony of the former Duke Zeibert's Restaurant, Duke himself shouted, "Come on up and have lunch – we have borscht!" Patrons crowded the rail.

People (including this author, her sister, and mother) jumped up on cars and helped others do the same for a better vantage point. A spontaneous cheer of "Gorby! Gorby!" rang out from the ground and from surrounding buildings. The commotion lasted for a few minutes until a KGB agent finally urged the leader back into his monstrous Zil limousine, and the motorcade moved on.

Gorbachev arrived at the White House over an hour late for his meeting with President Reagan, who greeted him at the door saying, "I thought you'd gone home!"

Address Connecticut Avenue, between K and L Streets NW, Washington, DC 20036 | **Getting there** Metro to Farragut North (Red Line); bus L 2, 42 to Connecticut Avenue NW and L Street NW; DC Circulator (Georgetown – Union Station Route) to K Street and Connecticut Avenue NW | **Hours** Unrestricted | **Tip** Stop in for a drink in Edgar's Bar in the Mayflower Hotel. It is named for regular J. Edgar Hoover, and it's where President Truman would look for Hoover when he wasn't in his office (1127 Connecticut Avenue NW, Washington, DC 20036).

47__Harriet Tubman's Shawl

Gift from a queen to a fearless warrior for freedom

Rarely has the accolade "hero" applied to anyone more aptly than to Harriet Tubman, or Moses, as she was known to enslaved people in the mid-1800s. Born into bondage on Maryland's Chesapeake Bay around 1822, Tubman escaped to freedom in 1849. Thus began her work as a conductor on the Underground Railroad, a clandestine system of hiding places and people who transported enslaved people to freedom in the North. She led 13 known trips of approximately 70 people from Maryland to Ontario.

Through the Civil War, she put her experience to use as a Union spy and was the first woman in US history to lead a military expedition. After the war, she became a suffragette. Later in life, she aided elderly and indigent formerly enslaved people.

Having heard of Tubman's exploits, Queen Victoria invited her to England for her Diamond Jubilee in 1897. Age and the expense kept Tubman from making the trip. So the queen sent a commendation letter, a silver medal, and a delicate silk shawl, one suitable for the monarch herself to have worn, as a show of respect and recognition of Tubman's fearless humanitarian work.

Philadelphia historian Charles L. Blockson, whose ancestors Moses had guided to freedom, inherited the shawl, one of few known items traceable directly back to her, and for years kept it hidden under his bed. You can see from its condition that she proudly wore and cherished it. Tubman's shawl now has a permanent place of honor in the Smithsonian's National Museum of African American History and Culture.

There is no underestimating Tubman's contributions to the greater good of American society. She was a friend to President Lincoln, notable abolitionists, politicians, and luminaries of the day, and yet she remained true to her roots and to her lifelong quest for freedom for all people. She lived by her will and her word.

Address National Museum of African American History and Culture, 1400 Constitution Avenue NW, Washington, DC 20560, +1 (844) 750-3012, www.nmaahc.si.edu | Getting there Metro to Federal Triangle (Blue, Orange, and Silver Line) | Hours Daily 10am–5:30pm | Tip The corona shape of the NMAAHC building was inspired by the crown on the head of a Yoruba wood carving by 19th-century Nigerian artist Olowe of Ise, which can be seen on the 4th floor in the Cultural Expressions gallery.

48 Hillwood Breakfast
Taste testing with Marjorie Merriweather Post

One of Marjorie Merriweather Post's favorite spots in her well-appointed, art-filled, Georgian mansion was the breakfast room, situated with a sunny 180-degree view of the Lunar lawn and the sensation of dining al fresco. The stunning landscaping changes seasonally, and the view towards the Washington Monument beyond the lawn adds to the scenery. The table was always set for four, and Marjorie served guests lunch and dinner there.

For her own breakfast, she preferred Postum, a breakfast drink and the first product of the Postum Cereal Company, later General Foods, which she inherited from her father. General Foods created new mass-produced foods in the 1950s through 1970s, and she loved to try out their products on her guests. She always inquired how the guests liked the food.

Marjorie was one of DC's foremost hostesses and philanthropists, and from the vast collection of menus, notes, and oral histories kept by her staff, it is clear that she only served the finest. Her staff prepared American meals served on her fine porcelain. She considered her table settings part of the art and décor that filled the house. Marjorie was most proud of Jello, and loved to serve it to guests in aspic salads and for dessert. She thought it was a very accessible food, and one of her favorites was blueberry Jello with tropical fruit. Instant General Foods International Coffees followed a meal.

When Post's father died and left her his company, she was the wealthiest woman in the world. She used much of her fortune to collect fine art, amassing one of the top private collections of French and pre-revolutionary Russian art, including Fabergé eggs from the Tsar's collection and jewelry once owned by monarchs.

A visit to Hillwood is a delight in any season, and it is fun to imagine that amidst the opulence of the surroundings, Jello was served for dessert.

Address Hillwood Estate, Museum, and Gardens, 4155 Linnean Street NW, Washington, DC 20008, +1 (202) 686-5807, www.hillwoodmuseum.org | Getting there Metro to Van Ness–UDC (Red Line); bus H 2, L 2 to Connecticut Avenue and Tilden Street NW | Hours Tue–Sun 10am–5pm | Tip Stroll down Tilden Street to the Pierce Mill, Spring House, and the Art Barn. During the Cold War, the pigeon coop in the barn was used as an FBI listening post to keep up with the goings-on at Soviet Bloc embassies across the street (2401 Tilden Street NW, Washington, DC 20008, www.nps.gov/places/peirce-mill.htm).

49 __ Howard Theatre

Where the greats have played

Shuttered and in decay from the 1980s to 2012, the Howard Theatre, once dubbed "the theater of the people," has risen again from its own ashes. Built in 1910 at the beginning of an era when theaters and movie palaces were going up all over the city, it began as a performance space for the Howard University Players, the Lafayette Players, and vaudeville and it was the largest colored theater in the world.

For those old enough to remember it in its heyday of the 1920s to 1950s, the Howard Theatre holds memories of weekends out, dressed to kill, to listen to the masters of music. Duke Ellington, Billie Holliday, Count Basie, Ella Fitzgerald, Pearl Bailey, Charlie Parker, Louis Armstrong, and their brethren all played there. Ellington was a regular.

During the height of segregation, which overlapped the Jazz Age, it was a venue for musicians and thespians of color to perform. The audiences were mixed, as there seemed no bounds for the appreciation of the "colored" music and theater that could be enjoyed there.

In the 1930s, an amateur contest helped launch the careers of Ella Fitzgerald and Billy Eckstine. Pearl Bailey debuted there in the 1940s. Raheem DeVaughn is a contemporary regular.

The building itself has changed hands many times and has been restored in a number of different styles. Gone is the opulent décor of the last century, but with change comes improved acoustics and cabaret-type balcony seating, perfectly positioned to see all the action on stage while receiving table service. As you enter, look up at Jazz Man, the glass and metal trumpeter standing atop the building.

Through fits and starts, the Howard remains one of the most iconic of American theaters, attracting renowned musicians who wish to play in more intimate settings and an even more diverse audience.

The spirit of the Greats pervades the building, inspiring all who perform there now and those who come for their performances.

Address 620 T Street NW, Washington, DC 20001, +1 (202) 803-2899, www.thehowardtheatre.com | **Getting there** Metro to Shaw–Howard Univ (Green and Yellow Line); bus 70 to 7th and T Streets NW | **Hours** See website for event schedule | **Tip** All of the proceeds from The Saloon go to building schools in underserved countries through the Kamal Foundation, and houses with Habitat for Humanity. On tap is one of the largest selections of German draft beer (1205 U Street NW, Washington, DC 20009, www.dcbeer.com/venue/saloon).

50 International Spy Museum

Spy pigeons and their covert critter colleagues

The oft defamed pigeon, or "flying rat," is vindicated in the International Spy Museum's exhibits on animal spies, along with actual rats, cats, and dragonflies. To this day, animal spy operations around the world have yet to be fully declassified.

The first known use by the US military of carrier pigeons, which possess an uncanny ability to return home, was during World War I. Trained birds would be released to fly ahead of advance ground troops to spot and land where they sighted oncoming enemy troops, signaling their locations. In World War II, British MI-14 parachuted crates of pigeons with questionnaires attached to them into occupied Europe. Over 1,000 pigeons returned to their homes with responses from Resistance fighters giving up enemy site locations and details of their situations on the ground.

During the Cold War, the CIA labs created highly acute mini cameras weighing a mere 40 grams that were strapped onto trained pigeons to be released near designated targets. The birds flew just a few hundred feet above a mark, and the cameras returned countless remarkably clear photos. Also of note in the museum are camera drones that look like dragonflies and stories of animal droppings used as cover for audio recording devices.

Meanwhile, domestic operatives and double agents resorted to leaving dead rats with the secret information stitched inside at designated drop spots. Unknowing humans left them alone, but the local cats fancied them for a meal. So the operatives resorted to dousing the rats with hot sauce to keep the hungry cats at bay.

Korean War code breaker Milton Maltz worked with a coterie of spies and intelligence officers from major global agencies to mastermind this impressive museum that strives to unveil the dark art of espionage and intelligence. Come with ample time to explore the exhibits, crawl through air ducts, and play spy craft games.

Flying spy pigeon with camera, Germany, 1914–1918

Address 700 L'Enfant Plaza SW, Washington, DC 20024, +1 (202) 393-7798, www.spymuseum.org, info@spymuseum.com | Getting there Metro to L'Enfant Plaza Station (Blue, Orange, Yellow, Green lines) | Hours Mon–Fri 10am–6pm; Sat 9am–7pm; Sun 9am–6pm | Tip Take a short walk to The Wharf to buy fun and saucy gifts of all kinds at woman-owned Diament Jewelry, where you can sit on swings while you sort through the goodies on tables in front of you (51 District Square SW, Washington, DC 20024, www.diamentjewelry.com).

51 Iron Gate Restaurant

A young hooker takes down a Soviet defector

Arkady Shevchenko was a Soviet diplomat and UN Undersecretary General, whose disdain for Soviet politics caused him resentment. From 1975 to 1978, he operated as a double agent, pressured by the CIA that promised asylum if he shared intelligence on the Soviet political agenda. He carried out his UN duties while doing the USSR's bidding inside the UN, and he passed Soviet cables to the CIA that enabled the US to decode valuable information. In 1978, he was summoned to Moscow for "consultation." Knowing that he was surely headed for trouble, he became the highest-ranking Soviet defector to the US.

Judy Chavez was a 22-year-old prostitute. Allegedly, Shevchenko requested a female companion, and a CIA agent picked a service out of the phone book. Shevchenko was her third trick of the day, and he kept inviting her back. She first received $500 for her services, and then a monthly retainer plus gifts. She treated him "viciously, but fairly."

One day, in tears, Shevchenko told her that his wife had died. The next day Chavez read about a defector's wife, taken to Moscow by the KGB, dying under suspicious circumstances. So his identity was fully exposed. That very day, she decided to write a book as an "insurance policy" to protect herself from possible CIA and KGB retribution. She hired a lawyer and a literary agent.

She next contacted NBC reporter Jim Polk, known for covering political corruption and fraud, asserting that she was paid with US taxpayers' money to service a Soviet defector. She set up a dinner date with Shevchenko at the cozy Iron Gate Inn. Instead of the prostitute, though, Polk and his camera crew turned up, exposing the tryst and blowing Shevchenko's cover. The CIA took Shevchenko back underground. The Iron Gate Inn remains a favorite haunt for journalists and politicians, as well as a Southern Comfort-loving ghost.

Address 1734 N Street NW, Washington, DC 20036, +1 (202) 524-5202, www.irongaterestaurantdc.com | Getting there Metro to Farragut North or Dupont Circle (Red Line); bus 42, L2 to Connecticut Avenue and 18th Street NW | Hours See website for hours | Tip After dinner, walk over to see the mural of Amanda Gorman, the first US Youth Poet Laureate, noted for her 2021 Presidential Inaugural poem, *The Hill We Climb* (1608 17th Street NW, Washington, DC 20009).

52 JFK Thank You Plaque
With gratitude from frozen newsmen

Directly across the street from 3307 N Street NW, the last home of John, Jackie, Caroline, and John Jr. Kennedy up until they moved into the White House in 1961, is a house with a plaque that reads:

"In the cold winter of 1960−61, this house had an important role in history. From it was flashed to the world news of pre-inaugural announcements by President John F. Kennedy. Presented by the grateful newsmen who were given warm haven here by Miss Helen Montgomery and her father, Charles Montgomery."

Through the brutally cold weather from Election Day through Inauguration Day over two months later, the press corps was camped out in front of Kennedy's unassuming Federal-style house, pending press conferences held on the steps of the home. Cabinet appointments and other news in the run-up to his swearing-in kept the press corps on their toes, even while they were turning to icicles.

Meanwhile, across the street, neighbor Helen Montgomery allowed the cold and weary journalists into her home to warm up and imbibe a little during their endless hours awaiting news. She offered them coffee, sandwiches, and the use of her phone and bathrooms. She even allowed them to install a few extra phone lines so that they could wire in their stories.

On the morning of his inauguration, President Kennedy himself walked across the street and presented the plaque from the newsmen to the Montgomerys with his and their deepest gratitude.

Just down Wisconsin Avenue is Martin's Tavern, where a reservation can get you the Proposal Booth, where Jack proposed to Jackie in 1953. JFK liked to grab breakfast alone here in the half booth – eggs Benedict with Smithfield ham or eggs over medium, bacon, rye toast, and hash browns, washed down with coffee and OJ. According to rumor, JFK had trysts at the home of his friend known as "the ringmaster of Camelot social life," at 2720 Dumbarton Street NW.

Address 3302 N Street NW, Washington, DC 20007 | Getting there Bus 31, 33, or DC Circulator (Union Station–Georgetown Route) to Wisconsin Avenue and N Street NW | Hours Unrestricted from outside only | Tip Janet Auchincloss, Jackie's mother, had Jackie's blood-spattered dress stored in her attic (3044 O Street NW, Washington, DC 20007) until she sent it to the National Archives in 1964. The dress now belongs to Caroline, who has a provision that the tragic relic not be displayed for at least a century.

53 John Philip Sousa Home
Marching with the spirits of great Washingtonians

Anyone who has ever played in a school marching band or attended a Fourth of July celebration is familiar with John Philip Sousa. It is hard to imagine fireworks in any American town without the accompanying refrains of his most famous piece, "Stars and Stripes Forever." Attending a US Marine Corps Band concert anywhere virtually ensures that you will hear at least one of his 137 marches.

The March King, as Sousa has been called, was a native Washingtonian whose childhood home on Capitol Hill was built in 1805 and is a private home to this day. The son of Portuguese and German immigrants, Sousa studied music from the age of six and played seven instruments. His father, a trombonist in the US Marine Corps Band, enlisted him at the age of 13 as an apprentice after he tried to run away to join a circus band. In 1880, he became the leader of the Marine Corps Band, The President's Own, serving under Presidents Hayes, Garfield, Arthur, Cleveland, and Harrison, the longest tenure of any Marine Corps bandleader. After his discharge in 1892, Sousa formed The Sousa Band and toured around the world until the year before his death in 1932. He is buried in nearby Congressional Cemetery.

Sousa was a prolific composer who wrote many operettas and other well-known music, including the official marches of the US Marine Corps and US Army, the Salvation Army, and "The Liberty Bell," later used as the theme song for the Monty Python's Flying Circus TV show. He also wrote three novels and an autobiography that was turned into a film in 1952.

Sousa's home is a detached, three-story, brick colonial typical of the era during which it was constructed. Today the iron railing has scrollwork in the shape of a lyre, a tribute to Sousa from a later resident, as well as an historical plaque installed near the entrance by the Capitol Hill Restoration Society in 1964.

Address 636 G Street SE, Washington, DC 20003 | Getting there Metro to Eastern Market (Blue, Orange, and Silver Line); bus 90, 92 to 8th and G Streets SE | Hours Unrestricted from the outside only | Tip Friday nights from May to August, the US Marine Corps Band, Drum and Bugle Corps, Color Guard, Silent Rifle Platoon, Ceremonial Guards, and Corporal Chesty, the bulldog mascot, offer a spectacle of marches and a silent rifle drill (8th and I Streets SE, Washington, DC 20003, www.barracks.marines.mil/Parades/Evening-Parade).

54 Julia Child's Kitchen
If you're afraid of butter, use cream

In 1976, Julia Child penned an essay for "Architectural Digest" and called her kitchen "the beating heart and social center of the household … both practical and beautiful, a working laboratory as well as a living and dining room." When you think of the legendary American chef, who specialized in classic French cooking, you might imagine that she made those stunning meals in an elaborate industrial style kitchen. In fact, everything had its place in her rather modest Cambridge, Massachusetts home kitchen, which doubled as the set for three of her beloved TV shows. Her husband Paul was integrally involved in the creation of her perfect kitchen. He drew outlines of pots, pans, and classic cast-iron skillets on the pegboards that hung on all the walls as a visual guide for which item went where. He hung his own art and that of friends, and he partnered with Julia in her every endeavor.

She was an avid gadget collector, and one of the first chefs to espouse the use of the food processor as a key tool. She loved knives and collected them in all types, arranged on magnetic racks by size and use. She used utensils dating from the 1940s and onward – she and Paul "rejoiced" in their shapes. Crockery jars for "Spoonery," "Spats," "Forkery," and "Wooden Things," creatively identifying the storage place for every tool.

The most notable chefs in the world cooked side by side with her in this kitchen, where they gave practical tips during demonstrations, made mistakes on live TV, laughed, talked about all things, and drank the occasional glass of wine that was paired with the meal on the stove. For 40 years, she taught and inspired viewers to embrace their creativity and to be fearless in the kitchen. Julia donated her entire kitchen to the Smithsonian Institution, and she was there on the day the exhibit opened in 2002 – just after her 90th birthday.

Address National Museum of American History, 1300 Pennsylvanian Avenue NW, Washington, DC 20560, +1 (202) 633-1000, www.americanhistory.si.edu/food/julia-childs-kitchen, info@si.edu | Getting there Metro to Federal Triangle (Blue, Orange, and Silver Line); bus 64, S2 to Constitution Avenue and 12th or 14th Streets NW | Hours 10am–5:30pm | Tip Now that you are inspired by Julia, head to Bold Fork Books for cookbooks and food memoirs in this well-stocked, food-only bookstore, and get to cooking! (3064 Mount Pleasant Street NW, Washington, DC 20009, www.boldforkbooks.com)

55 Kenilworth Aquatic Gardens

An age-old dance of wind, water, and land

Water lilies and lotuses are popular and related aquatic plants with a long history in Eastern and Egyptian culture and mythology. Water lilies, whose blooms hug the water line, conjure up visions of Monet's pond at Giverny. They are associated with rebirth and optimism, fertility, and spiritual enlightenment. The water lily is also the national flower of Bangladesh.

The lotus represents purity, reincarnation and rebirth in Buddhism, it is associated with the Hindu gods Laxmi and Brahma, and represents the sun in ancient Egyptian art and hieroglyphics. The stems and flowers of the lotus are emergent, rising above the water line, and the lotus is also known commonly for its seedpods.

Washington has a lasting connection to these aquatic plants. In 1882, Walter Shaw, a Civil War veteran, began planting aquatic plants in ponds he created on property he owned in marshlands adjoining the Anacostia River. Over the course of the next 40 years, he and his daughter Helen Shaw Fowler expanded the ponds and created a thriving business selling lilies, lotuses, and Japanese carp. They introduced several new varieties of lily, including ones named after Helen, and Shaw's wife Luciana. Walter Shaw died in 1921, and Congress purchased the property in 1938 to create Kenilworth Aquatic Gardens.

Today, Kenilworth Aquatic Gardens is maintained by the National Park Service as the only site devoted to aquatic plants. Along with the restored Kenilworth Marsh, the Gardens are part of Kenilworth Park, which sits directly across the river from the National Arboretum at the northeast edge of the District. Open year round, the Gardens are great for short hikes. Violets bloom in April, and water lilies and lotuses in summer. Over 40 species of aquatic, woodland, and ground birds make for a good day of birding any time of year.

Address 1550 Anacostia Avenue NE, Washington, DC 20019, +1 (202) 692-6080, www.nps.gov/keaq/index.htm | Getting there Metro to Deanwood (Orange Line), cross Kenilworth Avenue NE at the pedestrian bridge, to Douglas Street NE, right onto Anacostia Avenue NE to any open gate; bus U7 to Kenilworth Avenue and Douglas Street NE | Hours See website for seasonal hours | Tip The week-long Annual Lotus and Water Lily Festival takes place in July. The family-friendly event features food, entertainment, and vendors from around the world (www.nps.gov/keaq/planyourvisit/lotus-and-water-lily-festival.htm).

56 Key Bridge Boathouse
Paddling on the Potomac

The Potomac River is called the wildest river in the world that flows through a busy urban area. But your experience can be fabulous and not so wild.

The Key Bridge, named for Francis Scott Key, composer of the "Star Spangled Banner," carried its first vehicles between Georgetown in DC and Rosslyn in Northern Virginia in 1923. In the shadow of its arches lies the Key Bridge Boathouse.

Paddlers can rent canoes, kayaks, and paddleboards. The Boathouse also offers lessons for beginners. You can take a daytime, twilight, or nighttime guided tour of the monuments that are visible from the waterfront, including the Lincoln Memorial, the Kennedy Center for Performing Arts, and the notorious Watergate. Each year between mid-March to mid-April, you can take a spectacular cherry blossom boating tour. Check the weather before you go, and make your reservation online well in advance.

Washington, DC is a city of great natural beauty, and the Potomac River is its crowning glory. From the Boathouse, you can paddle all around Roosevelt Island. You can paddle along the lively Georgetown waterfront, and over to The Three Sisters Islands.

The Three Sisters are three tiny, rocky islands in a deep channel of the Potomac just north of Key Bridge. They get their name from an Algonquin story of three sisters who perished in the river while attempting to save their brothers from captivity by another tribe. Upon their deaths, the sisters' bodies turned into these small islands. It is said that they are haunted, emitting an eerie sound when a boater is in trouble. On a warm, sunny day, though, it's just nice to point your boat's nose towards these pretty little islets.

Key Bridge boathouse is one of seven boathouses in DC, each offering different activities and views. Check the Boating In DC website for locations, services, fees, and weather conditions.

Address 3500 Water Street NW, Washington, DC 20007, +1 (202) 337-9642, www.boatingindc.com/boathouses/key-bridge-boathouse, dcboatinginfo@boatingindc.com | Getting there Metro to Foggy Bottom–GWU (Blue, Orange, and Silver Line); bus 31, 33 to M and 31st Streets NW | Hours See website for seasonal hours | Tip Learn to row or paddle, or join a masters team at the Anacostia Community Boathouse (1900 M Street SE, Washington, DC 20003, www.anacostiaboathouse.org).

57 KGB Double Agent Escape
Where spy met spy

The former Au Pied du Cochon Restaurant in Georgetown, now Greco, is where KGB Agent Vitaly Yurchenko had his last dinner in DC with his neophyte CIA handler. Yurchenko had defected to the United States three months earlier in 1985, to the chagrin of the Soviet Union. At the time, he was one of the highest-ranking spymasters in the KGB, responsible for all spy activity in the US and Canada and had been a diplomat in Washington in the 1970s. Yurchenko was a master of the "dangle," or inserting spies into foreign, particularly US, intelligence operations, generally in the guise of diplomats.

He made his CIA handler believe that he had turned defector to the CIA. But on that last day, he asked, "What would you do if I got up and walked out of here? Would you shoot me?" The response was "No, we don't treat defectors that way." He replied, "I will be back in 15 or 20 minutes. If I am not, it is not your fault." With that, Yurchenko climbed out a bathroom window and made his way through the bustle of Georgetown to a suspected tunnel into the Soviet Embassy a few blocks up the street. Within a few days, he turned up at a rare news conference making a mockery of the US, and shortly after he was back in Moscow. It remains unclear to this day whether he was a double agent or a plant by the KGB. There is a theory that he was sent to embarrass the CIA and to compromise the political climate in the run-up to the November 1985 summit between Presidents Ronald Reagan and Mikhail Gorbachev. His glory would not endure, however. His last known sighting was in a Moscow bank, where he was working as a security officer.

The restaurant in DC capitalized on the publicity by serving a Yurchenko Shooter made of Stolichnaya vodka and Grand Marnier. They marked the bench where he always sat with a brass plaque, which was sadly removed by the current occupant.

Address 1335 Wisconsin Avenue NW, Washington, DC 20007, +1 (202) 499-3600, www.grecotrulygreek.com | Getting there Metro to Foggy Bottom–GWU (Blue, Orange, and Silver Line); bus 31, 33 to Wisconsin Avenue and Dumbarton Street NW | Hours Unrestricted from the outside | Tip Aldrich Ames walked into what is now Mrs. Smith's of Georgetown and handed classified documents revealing the locations and actions of US spies in the USSR to the Soviet Embassy's chief of counterintelligence, one of the greatest intelligence breaches in US history (3205 K Street NW, Washington, DC, 20007, www.mrsmiths.com).

58 Khalil Gibran Memorial

Beauty shall rise with the dawn

One of the most serene spots in the District is a small garden dedicated to peace and understanding in memory of the Lebanese-American poet and philosopher Khalil Gibran. Gibran was a Maronite Christian born in Lebanon in 1883 who, at age 12, immigrated to the United States with his mother and siblings. He was an accomplished artist, having attended the Académie Julian art school in Paris, and more importantly an influential poet and storyteller of parables and aphorisms, first in Arabic, then later in English. Gibran died of cirrhosis and tuberculosis in 1931, but his work has long outlived him. He was particularly popular during the 1930s and the 1960s, referenced by the likes of The Beatles, JFK, David Bowie, and Indira Gandhi.

His best-known work, *The Prophet*, sometimes called "the bible of counterculture," has sold millions of copies in over 100 languages since its publication in 1923, has never been out of print, and is credited with introducing generations of people to Eastern mysticism.

The book tells the story of holy man Al Mustafa whom people gather around to ask for words of wisdom. He provides counsel on a range of topics, from friendship to marriage to time, in a pan-religious manner that comforts readers seeking the insight of religions without owing allegiance to any god or church.

The 2-acre Khalil Gibran Memorial across from the British Embassy was dedicated by President George Bush and members of the Lebanese community in 1991. A footbridge leads to a bust of Gibran with laurel branches and doves by sculptor Gordon Kray. Beyond that, a small circular plaza with star-shaped flagstones and a fountain is surrounded by stone benches inscribed with some of Gibran's best known quotes: "Life without freedom is like a body without a soul and freedom without thought is confusion," and "We live only to discover beauty. All else is a form of waiting."

Address Woodland-Normanstone Terrace Park, Massachusetts Avenue NW, between 30th Street and Observatory Circle NW, Washington, DC 20008 | **Getting there** Bus N 2, N 4, N 6 to Massachusetts Avenue and 30th Street NW | **Hours** Unrestricted | **Tip** Two world leaders are honored with statues opposite one another. Winston Churchill stands with one foot on British soil, that of the Embassy (3100 Massachusetts Avenue NW, Washington, DC 20008). Nelson Mandela stands before the Embassy of South Africa (3051 Massachusetts Avenue NW, Washington, DC 20008).

59__LeDroit Park

A historic bastion of African-American influencers

Tucked between U Street and Howard University is the tiny enclave of LeDroit Park. Set off from the DC street grid intentionally to keep out non-residents, local developer James McGill built 64 homes in the 1870s, of which 50 remain. The diversity of the neighborhood's architectural styles – Queen Anne, Victorian, Italianate, Second Empire and Carriage – would be impossible now, given modern zoning rules. From its origin as a gated, all-white community, it evolved into a bastion of influential black residents after protests resulted in the removal of the gate in the 1890s.

At 525 T Street, the owner rented rooms to black musicians performing at the Howard Theatre and disallowed from segregated hotels. Rumor persists that there was a tunnel connecting the house and the theatre to enable musicians to avoid the crowds outside. The theatre has said that there is a mysterious hole in the basement, though it is yet to be explored.

The House of Secrets at 507 T Street has been a speakeasy and an underground music spot throughout its history. Prince was snuck in to perform twice in the 1990s. Getting an invitation is as mysterious as the stories themselves.

Former LeDroit Park residents include Ernest Everett Just, a pioneering Howard University biologist who resided at 412 T Street and whose discoveries in cell behavior earned him world renown, and DC's first elected mayor, Walter E. Washington, who resided at 408 T Street. Older locals recall that his house was one of their favorites on Halloween. Mary Church Terrell, a suffragette and founding member of the NAACP, lived with her husband Robert Terrell, DC's first black judge, at 326 T Street. One of the most stunning homes, replete with an enclosed gazebo on the porch, belonged to Anna Julia Cooper, the fourth African-American woman to earn a PhD at the Sorbonne and principal of the M Street High School.

Address Entrance sign at 6th and T Streets NW, Washington, DC 20001, www.ledroitparkdc.org | **Getting there** Metro to Shaw–Howard Univ (Green and Yellow Line); bus 90, 92 to Florida Avenue and 6th Street NW | **Hours** Unrestricted | **Tip** From 1891 to 1961, several teams played baseball in an evolving series of fields and stadiums at the intersection of Georgia and Florida Avenues. The most notable was the former Griffiths Stadium, now the site of Howard University Hospital, where on April 18, 1953, Mickey Mantle hit a 565-foot home run, the longest ever measured.

60 Letelier-Moffitt Memorial
Assassination on Embassy Row

On September 21, 1976, in front of the Embassy of Romania, a car bomb detonated, killing former Chilean Ambassador to the US Orlando Letelier and his colleague Ronni Karpen Moffitt. The assassination that left witnesses in shock at the gruesome scene was carried out by hitmen hired by the Chilean military dictator Augusto Pinochet to silence the outspoken critic of his regime. Moffitt was in the car with her husband Michael, who survived the attack.

Letelier, who had been living in Washington, was appointed as ambassador to the US in 1971 by socialist president Salvador Allende. Recalled to Chile in early 1973, he held three cabinet positions. After the 1973 military coup led by Pinochet to overthrow Allende, Letelier was arrested and tortured for a year until the regime was forced to release him under heavy worldwide pressure. He returned to Washington, DC in exile and worked at the progressive Institute for Policy Studies.

The bombing was part of Operation Condor, a covert terror operation of several Latin American right-wing dictatorships to silence leftist intellectuals, Communists, and subversives, chiefly those with a loud public voice. The FBI and other global agencies found indications that Pinochet himself had ordered the hit. Over the course of 40 years, numerous players, including the head of the Chilean Secret Police, were indicted in international courts, though Pinochet was never prosecuted. Until 9/11, it was considered the most treacherous act of international state-sponsored terrorism in the US.

The memorial, a medallion on a round stone base, was dedicated five years after the assassination and marks the spot where the bomb exploded. Every year family, friends and human rights advocates gather on the Sunday closest to the anniversary to pay tribute to both victims and to bring light to ongoing human rights issues throughout the world.

ORLANDO LETELIER

JUSTICE - PEACE - DIGNITY

APR. 13, 1932 - SEPT. 21, 1976

RONNI K. MOFFITT JAN. 10, 1951 - SEPT. 21, 1976

Address Sheridan Circle between Massachusetts Avenue and 23rd Street NW, Washington, DC 20008 | Getting there Metro to Dupont Circle (Red Line), Q Street exit, walk two blocks west, right on Massachusetts Avenue NW, left at Sheridan Circle | Hours Unrestricted | Tip Stop in the Woodrow Wilson House Museum (2340 S Street NW, Washington, DC 20008) home of the only president to stay in DC until Barack Obama, who lives nearby. Amazon's Jeff Bezos bought the former Textile Museum next door (2320 S Street NW).

61 Lincoln Life Masks

A civil war can change the face of a man

The face of a president at the end of his term often looks quite different from his early days in office. Sometimes the change is shocking, perhaps none more than the face of President Abraham Lincoln, who presided over the Civil War.

Using wet plaster on the face of a subject to capture the person's features in life or in death was common in the 18th and 19th centuries. The molds were often used to cast metal likenesses.

Prior to Lincoln's nomination in 1860 as the Republican presidential candidate, he was reminded by artist Leonard Wells Volk of a prior promise to sit for a face mask so that a bust could later be cast. The mold stuck firmly, thanks to his high cheekbones. He spent some time getting it off, losing a few eyebrow hairs in the process. His features were robust and hearty, those of a man of character ready to take on the leadership of a still fledgling nation in a precarious time. The life mask, one of two in the National Portrait Gallery, is a replica cast in 1917 from the original mold.

In May 1869, Volk cast Lincoln's hands holding a broom handle (to simulate a document) for a life-size statue. You can see that his right hand is swollen from shaking so many hands, and the left thumb scarred by his days on the railroad.

Clark Mills made the second mask in February 1865. The bearded, gaunt, sorrowful face appears to be a death mask; Lincoln would live for just two more months. It reflects the toll that the war and its consequences had taken.

After Lincoln's death, editor Richard Watson Gilder gathered friends, including sculptor Augustus St. Gaudens, to buy the original cast to give to the National Museum (now the National Museum of American History). He wrote, "This bronze doth keep the very form and mold of our great martyr's face…" St. Gaudens supervised production of bronze and plaster casts, sold to pay for the museum donation.

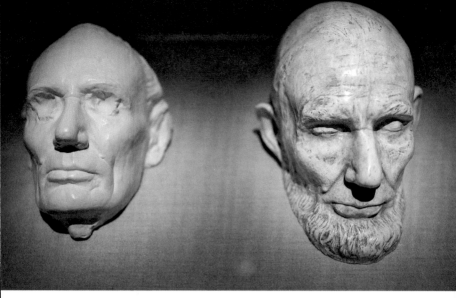

Address National Portrait Gallery, 8th and F Streets NW, Washington, DC 20001, +1 (202) 633-8300, www.npg.si.edu | **Getting there** Metro to Gallery Pl–Chinatown (Red, Yellow, and Green Line); bus 42 to 9th and F Streets NW, or bus 80, P 6, X 2 to H and 9th Streets NW | **Hours** Daily 11:30am–7pm | **Tip** Every Tuesday from 12:10 to 1pm, there is a free concert at the Church of the Epiphany. Most artists are locals who apply to perform predominantly classical music (1317 G Street NW, Washington, DC 20005, www.epiphanydc.org/epiphanies-happen/concerts).

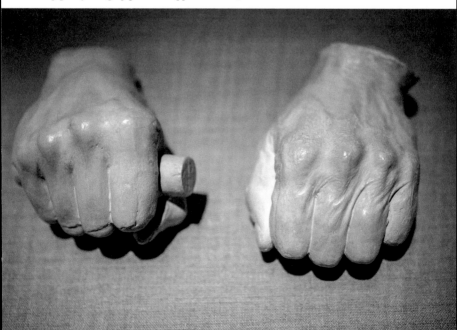

62 Lincoln's Cottage

He wrote the Emancipation Proclamation here

"What does it mean to be brave?" is the question asked at the beginning of the tour. This elegant summer cottage was built by banker George Riggs in 1842, and in 1851 sold to the government for use as a soldiers' retirement home. By 1857, the retirees were moved to new larger quarters and the house was offered to President Buchanan as a retreat. President Abraham Lincoln was later invited to use the home as his summer cottage, which he gladly accepted, to escape the heat of the swamp that was downtown and the ghost of his son Willy who had recently died in the White House. He availed himself of the cottage in the summers of 1862 to 1864. As original furnishings were sold off over time and never found, the empty rooms are now filled not with furniture, but rather with remarkable stories.

Each day, President Lincoln would ride his horse the 40 minutes from the cottage to the White House to put in his day's work. He enjoyed the ride and used the time to try to relax and ponder the business of the day. On one of his daily rides, a sniper took a shot at him, leaving a hole in his stovepipe hat. In September 1862, he was given an armed cavalry escort, which he frequently took pleasure in evading.

Lincoln's trusted service staff kept diaries of the goings-on at the cottage, and butler William Slade wrote letters to the President with his comments about the Emancipation Proclamation. The desk upon which Lincoln penned the final draft of this historic document through most of 1862 was moved to the White House by President Hoover and remains in the Lincoln bedroom. On January 1, 1863, the document that ended slavery in the US was read for the first time, declaring "that all persons held as slaves" within the rebellious states "are, and henceforward shall be free."

Lincoln's last visit to the cottage was April 13, 1865, the day before he was shot at Ford's Theatre.

Address Armed Forces Retirement Home (AFRH), Eagle Gate, 140 Rock Creek
Church Road NW, Washington, DC 20011, +1 (202) 829-0436, www.lincolncottage.org,
info@lincolncottage.org | Getting there Metro to Georgia Avenue–Petworth (Green
and Yellow Line) and walk 0.9 miles along Rock Creek Church Road NW; bus H8 to
Rock Creek Church Road and Upshur Street NW | Hours Daily 9:30am–4:30pm | Tip
During Black History Month each February, the National Archives puts the Emancipation
Proclamation on display for only 3 days (Constitution Avenue at 9th Street NW,
Washington, DC 20408, www.archives.gov/museum).

63 The Longest Protest
Civic action facing the White House

As the nation's capital, Washington has a long history of protests and marches. 5,000 marched for women's suffrage in 1913. 75,000 attended a concert at the Lincoln Memorial by African-American opera singer Marian Anderson in 1939. The 1963 March on Washington was a pivotal moment in the civil rights movement. 600,000 gathered on the Mall in 1969 to protest the Vietnam War. In recent decades, huge demonstrations called for gay rights, women's rights, pro- and anti-abortion rights, gun control, and the end to various wars.

One small protest, however, can be called the longest running protest in Washington history. The Peace Vigil was started by William Thomas and Concepción Piciotto in 1981, in the middle of the Cold War, and Thomas' wife Ellen joined them soon after. Several close calls between the United States and the Soviet Union inspired Thomas to start the vigil, and despite efforts to have it removed and occasional attacks by people angered by its message, the tent, chairs, hand-painted peace and anti-war signs, and donation bucket remain to this day.

Any visitor to the area in Lafayette Square directly in front of the White House over the past over 40 years will have seen the vigil, and many will have spoken to its volunteers. In addition to its anti-nuclear focus, the Peace Vigil has staged protests against the Gulf War, Iraq War, and the Syrian War, and has participated in many other campaigns for peace. To this day, no American president has acknowledged or visited the encampment.

William Thomas died in 2009, Ellen Thomas left the vigil shortly thereafter, and Concepcion Piciotto died in 2016. It looked like the Peace Vigil had come to an end, but a new group of protest volunteers has taken up the cause. Recently, the Peace Vigil signs have added other themes, but the spirit and determination of the founders still remain for all to witness.

Address Lafayette Square at 1600 Pennsylvania Avenue NW, Washington, DC 20006 |
Getting there Metro to Farragut North (Red Line), Farragut West or MacPherson Square
(Blue, Orange, and Silver Line); bus 32, 33, 36, G8 to H Street and Madison Place NW |
Hours Unrestricted | Tip Stan's Restaurant is a neighborhood joint that has been serving
no-frills, affordable cocktails for decades. Order a gin and tonic, a highball of gin on the
rocks with a small bottle of tonic on the side. The drinks are good and strong (1029 Vermont
Avenue NW, Washington, DC 20005, www.stansrestaurant.com).

64 Longest City Bus Tour
The $2 city tour

You can take an expansive city tour for a mere $2. The combined 33 and 36 bus routes offer the longest ride from end to end in under two hours. The ride runs from Friendship Heights in upper NW to Naylor Road across the far NE border. Board the 33 bus at Friendship Heights metro station and sit on the driver's side for the best sightings.

Majestic National Cathedral, the sixth largest Gothic cathedral in the world, is spectacularly poised atop St. Albans Hill and resplendent when the sun is high in the West. At the next block begins Embassy Row on Massachusetts Avenue, a great 2.5-mile walk down to Dupont Circle. Down on the right is the Russian Embassy complex, strategically poised for a listening post. On Sundays, stop at the Georgetown Flea Market, across from the "Social Safeway," the grocery store that was once the place to mingle in the frozen food section. Georgetown bustles with colorful shops and elegant old architecture.

Across from the World Bank, the Normandy Hotel's genie bottle-style bar and the Arts Club are relaxing stops. Further along, Lafayette Park is home to ghosts, spy stories, St. John's "Church of the Presidents," and a view of the White House's north entrance.

Transfer from Route 33 to 36 at Pennsylvania Avenue and 10th Street NW to complete the ride. On Pennsylvania Avenue, median traffic signals magically disappear for the presidential inaugural parade every four years. As the bus crosses the National Mall, you'll see the Capitol, Smithsonian Castle, and Washington Monument, all beautifully framed through your window, especially at twilight.

On Capitol Hill, pass the Botanical Garden, US Capitol, Libraries of Congress, Eastern Market, and Barracks Row. Once your bus crosses the Sousa Bridge, the view is mostly residential and a bit dicey in some spots, so hop off at Potomac Avenue to explore Congressional Cemetery.

Address Friendship Heights Station, Western and Wisconsin Avenues NW and Naylor Road Station, Naylor Road and Branch Avenue, Hillcrest Heights, MD (at DC line), www.wmata.com/schedules/maps | Getting there Begin at Friendship Heights Metro Station Bus Bay C. Take Bus 31 towards West Potomac Park to Virginia Avenue & E Street NW. Transfer to bus 36 towards Naylor Road Metro Station. Or begin at Naylor Road Metro Station Bus Bay F and do the reverse. | Hours Daily 5am–midnight | Tip Mr. Henry's, one of the oldest establishments in DC to welcome members of the LGBTQIA+ community, is a notable stop for jazz and other live music from Thursday to Saturday. Roberta Flack once was a regular performer (601 Pennsylvania Avenue SE, Washington, DC 20003, www.mrhenrysdc.com).

65 — The Magic Tree Box

A fairy world at your feet

It's easy to miss the marvels that are not in your direct line of sight. So look down to see the joyful, knee-high Magic Tree Box.

This lilliputian village built around a beautiful old tree is the clever creation of Art Hahn, engineer by trade, miniature landscape architect by calling, and driven by creativity and experimentation. Inspired by movies (can you guess which ones?), Pinterest, and *wabi-sabi*, the village began with boxes and twigs. Some objects come and go or get moved around, such as animals, produce, cars, and décor. Visit often to see what's new or different.

The red door on the east side of the tree in Fairy Valley, the first place ever graced by a fairy, was placed after an unsuccessful series of attempts to grow a flower garden. Kneel down and look closely, and you may see a pair of tiny Vespas at the ready, a bench made of twigs for enjoying a beautiful day, a unicorn, mushrooms live and handmade, and lovely little houses that may be aglow with indoor lighting at twilight.

On the west side, across the babbling brook that actually flows with water periodically, thanks to an ingenious concealed contraption, you'll find Hobbit Hill with hobbit houses throughout, most furrowed into the hillsides, front and back. The blue-doored Mayor's House is the biggest in the Shire, where the fairies enjoy moving and replacing décor on the porch and around the yard – perhaps a pumpkin today and a VW bus in the driveway tomorrow.

In cold weather, the fairies light their fireplaces, and real smoke might be seen coming from the tiny chimneys. And do you see the bunny in the window of the house on the tree trunk? It is behind the handmade shade.

Hahn joyfully states, "It is always new, different and changing, but only to the person paying attention. The magic is there if you see it. If you allow yourself to see it." So stop and look!

Address 1429 R Street NW, Washington DC 20009, www.instagram.com/
the_magic_tree_box | **Getting there** Metro to Dupont Circle (Red Line), walk 0.8 miles,
or bus 52, 54 to 14th and R Streets NW | **Hours** Unrestricted | **Tip** On a grand scale,
the Moorish and Romanesque Cairo building (1615 Q Street NW) was once the tallest
residential building and hotel that was partially the reason for the height restriction
of DC's buildings.

66 Maine Avenue Fish Market

Crabs, oysters, and fried fish sammiches

In business since 1805, the Fish Market is the oldest continuously operating open-air fish market in the US, floating on several barges that are moored to the wharf. With a new adjacent development, the market will experience some modernizations, yet it will retain its charms and character. It is long anchored by Jessie Taylor's Seafood, which offers a vast array of regionally caught and imported fish and shrimp, which range from tiny to gigantic. In season, farm fresh produce is also on the menu.

Enjoy your share of the ubiquitous Maryland blue crab in the form of lump crabmeat in a container, or, more fun, by the bushel or partial bushel, live for the picking. Each purveyor can steam shellfish on site in a few minutes, or you can take them home and cook them yourself. Not to be overlooked is the native Old Bay Seasoning that locals can't serve seafood, especially crabs, without. Though the fishermen no longer come up the Potomac River directly to the barges, the food is trucked in daily from all over the Eastern Seaboard. If you are on the move, purchase a meal to go at most vendors, whether shellfish, spiced shrimp, or a fried whiting "sammich." There is limited seating, but you can walk a couple of blocks and find a table at the new wharf.

Sam, a long-time shucker at Jessie Taylor's, can offer you oysters on the half shell in no time. Most of the shellfish comes from the Chesapeake Bay region, but occasionally they offer variations from North Carolina, the Gulf of Mexico, and Canada. Sam muses that women always ask for the biggest oysters – more meat for the same price. The best time for heavy, meaty crabs is from August to November, which, coincidentally, is when they are cheaper. In summer they molt, so there is less meat in a larger shell. He also has a no-fail oyster stew recipe that you can make at home in plastic bags in a matter of minutes. Just ask.

Address 1100 Maine Avenue SW, Washington, DC 20024, +1 (202) 484-2722 | Getting there Metro to Waterfront (Green Line), walk along the channel to the wharf; bus 52 to Maine Avenue and 7th Street SW | Hours Mon–Thu 10am–8pm, Fri 9am–8pm, Sat & Sun 8am–8pm | Tip Take in a play or a rousing musical at Arena Stage, the first ever to win the Tony Award for Best Regional Theater. (1101 6th Street SW, Washington, DC 20024, www.arenastage.org).

67 Mansion on O Street

Wonder, through secret doorways

This marvel of a place dedicated to creativity in every possible form is an ever-changing kaleidoscope of art, music, chandeliers, furnishings, and unimaginable trinkets and treasures. H.H. Leonards Spero, the proprietor, was assisted in creating this vibrant culture center and upscale discreet inn by a seatmate on a flight many years ago. She told him of her vision for her creative enterprise and prior to the end of the flight he handed her a crumpled check for $40,000. He later told her it was a gift, with the stipulation that she must pay it forward, a promise she fulfills to her DC community.

Over the years, H purchased and connected five row houses built by the fifth architect of the US Capitol, Edward Clark, and maintained the ornate woodwork created by German craftsmen who stayed at his home during his tenure. At first pass, you see the obvious, but look closer. One of the greatest pleasures of a visit is the search for over 80 secret doorways. They are tougher to find than you may imagine, but the search brings delight and even a competitive zeal. "I am above average – I found two doors!" said a happy visitor.

Simply going to the bathroom may protract "taking a powder" while you read the "dry cleaning" letter to John Lennon, marvel at the lacquered wood tub, sit on a piano, or try to figure out how to get into the London phone-booth shower. In the event rooms, the ceilings are bright with painted clouds and sparkly stamped tin tiles. Stained-glass windows and chandeliers add colorful effects. Most items may be bought with the exception of the collection of signed guitars from a who's who of musicians. Each of the 100 rooms has its distinct theme and décor, and the inventory changes frequently, so if something speaks to you, take the plunge.

Come on event days for intimate concerts, brunch, scavenger hunts, and holiday festivities. Creativity and wonder abound.

Address 2020 O Street NW, Washington, DC 20036, www.omansion.com | **Getting there** Metro to Dupont Circle (Red Line); bus D 6 to New Hampshire Avenue and O Street NW | **Hours** Sun & Mon 9am–6pm, Tue & Sat 9am–9pm, with tour reservation | **Tip** In cold weather the fireplace adds to the coziness of the Tabard Inn's bar, and in warm weather the patio seating is divine. The food and drink at the oldest, continuously operating hotel in DC are worthy of a visit at any time. Reservations are suggested for meals (1739 N Street NW, Washington, DC 20036. www.tabardinn.com).

68__The Market Lunch

Blue bucks for breakfast

Back in the day, if you were lucky, one of the line cooks at this favorite neighborhood joint might be enticed to sing "Happy Birthday" to a customer in line. There was nothing like a gospel voice to fire up the crowd for a hearty breakfast.

The Market Lunch counter is best known for its signature breakfast and lunch offerings. Blue Bucks, or blueberry buckwheat pancakes to the layman, can be had in a short (2) or full (3) stack, each the size of a small plate, served with real maple syrup. Either stack will fill you up and make you happy for the entire day. The Brick, an immense sandwich of egg, meat, cheddar cheese, and potato on a house-baked roll, is not for the faint of heart or stomach. A crabcake sandwich or a selection of fried fish sandwiches will give you that protein boost you need to get through your day. Have your cash ready (no credit cards) and your order on the tip of your tongue, as the line moves quickly.

The affable staff will have your food ready in no time.

This small lunch counter, in business since 1978, is situated in a busy corner inside historic Eastern Market. Owner Tommy Glasgow started out as a 22-year-old entrepreneur with the guidance of chef Lonnie Brown, creator of most of the recipes, which remain in use today. Eastern Market was part of Pierre L'Enfant's original plan for the city, which included an array of markets to serve many neighborhoods. It is the sole survivor, and has been in continuous operation since 1873. A 3-alarm fire in April 2007 almost destroyed it. A makeshift space was set up in an adjacent lot to keep the farmers, and craft and vintage vendors in business. Luckily, a public-private partnership restored the market to its historic grandeur, with a few modern amenities added. In just over two years, it was open and back to normal. After your pancakes, head out to shop the rest of the market. Get there early on weekends!

Address Inside Eastern Market, 225 7th Street SE, Washington, DC 20003, +1 (202) 547-8444, www.marketlunchdc.com | Getting there Metro to Eastern Market (Orange, Blue, and Silver Line); bus 32, 36 to Pennsylvania Avenue and 8th Street SE | Hours Tue–Thu 8am–2:15pm, Fri & Sat 8am–2:30pm, Sun 9am–2:30pm | Tip Capitol Hill is full of alley dwellings. Check out Browns, Walker, and Library Courts in SE, and the other charming alley neighborhoods (www.sellingdc.com/blog/alley-life-on-capitol-hill.html).

69 Mexican Cultural Institute
Stairway to vibrant colors and rich traditions

Be sure to check out all the stations at the recently refreshed Mitsitam Native Foods Cafe at the Smithsonian's National Museum of the American Indian. Campfire Grill, Mitsitam Chef's Table, The Four Corners, and Woodlands & Coastlines stations offer dishes made from recipes and indigenous foods sourced from across the Americas, from northmost Canada to southernmost Argentina. Executive Chef Alexandra Strong and Sous Chef Toshiba Veney are the first all–female duo to lead the kitchen of a Smithsonian cafe and are carrying forth what their predecessors began.

Founding Chef Richard Hetzler established the café as a forerunner in the research and offering of Native dishes and wrote a cookbook showcasing its bounty. Then, Chef Freddie Bitsoie, Diné (Navajo), established an anthropological perspective for the food, encouraging every effort to research traditional recipes, ingredients, and their histories. Staying true to the traditions of the food is the key to the menus here. Food and storytelling go hand in hand in Native culture, whether the stories are about the food itself or told while cooking it.

Menus rotate each season, combining opposite seasons of the northern and southern hemispheres, which allows the serving of southern summer produce simultaneously with northern winter items, and vice versa. Special foods are served for festivals, fairs, and holidays that may be taking place in the museum or in the Americas, such as Day of the Dead and an annual Chocolate Festival.

"Mitsitam" means "Let's Eat" in the language of the Piscataway and Delaware people of this region. Among the staples here are planked salmon, bison burgers, and fry bread. Tribes have an ongoing discussion over whose fry bread recipe is best, and if you haven't tried it yet, start here. The stars of the menu are the uncommon and delicious seasonal dishes that keep locals coming back.

Address 2829 16th Street NW, Washington, DC 20009, +1 (202) 728-1628, www.instituteofmexicodc.org, culturemexico@instituteofmexicodc.org | Getting there Bus S 2, S 4 to 16th and Euclid Streets NW, or bus H 2 to Columbia Road and 16th Street NW | Hours Mon–Fri 10am–6pm, Sat noon–4pm, closed on major US and Mexican holidays | Tip Take a stroll through Meridian Hill Park, located on the exact longitude of the original 1791 milestone marker for DC at 16th and Euclid Streets. The 13-basin fountain is the longest in North America, and Joan of Arc is the only female equestrian statue in the city.

70 Millennium Stage
Free entertainment 365 days a year Nearly every

day of the year at 6pm on one of the two Millennium Stages in the Grand Foyer of The John F. Kennedy Center for the Performing Arts, there is live music or dance, plus a livestream. For free. This is the only performing arts center in the country where everyone has access to a free performance on any given day.

The Kennedy Center was created by President Dwight D. Eisenhower with the National Culture Center Act. John F. Kennedy continued the vision and was the leading proponent and fundraiser for its development. After his assassination, it was renamed for him as a living memorial that opened in 1971 and includes a theater named for President Eisenhower. Most of the décor was gifted by other nations. A guide to the gifts is available at the information desk.

Imagined by the team of former Kennedy Center chairman James A. Johnson, the Millennium Stage performances began in 1999 as part of the mission to provide access to the arts for all.

An impressive array of styles and genres of music, dance, and performing arts grace these stages. Whether a high-school dance troupe from across the country, internationally known Big Bad Voodoo Daddy or Chopteeth, or an Indigenous or international group that is part of an arts festival bringing the flavors of their cultures, there are always wondrous and surprising performances. Annual favorites are the National Symphony Orchestra, Merry Tuba Christmas, and National Dance Day with dancers from So You Think You Can Dance leading a dance class. Anniversary parties on March 19 are not to be missed. Big shows may be moved into one of the theaters or outdoors to The Reach Plaza to accommodate larger crowds.

No matter your taste in performing arts, the Millennium Stage has it all, and undoubtedly some special shows that will get your toes tapping, make you marvel at unusual talent, or broaden your horizons.

Address 2700 F Street NW, Washington, DC 20566, +1 (202) 467-4600, www.kennedy-center.org | Getting there Metro to Foggy Bottom–GWU (Blue, Orange, and Silver Line) and then take Kennedy Center shuttle which runs every 15 minutes; bus 42 to Kennedy Center | Hours See website for performance and tour schedules | Tip House of Sweden is the public diplomacy branch of the Swedish Embassy. Public exhibits and events that represent Swedish culture are held regularly in this very hospitable embassy (2900 K Street NW, Washington, DC 20007, www.houseofsweden.com).

71 Missing Soldiers Office
Fate lent a hand – and a letter – to save history

Clara Barton had been a copyist at the US Patent Office, but after losing her job over political views, she had grand ideas of providing humanitarian aid to those in need. She established the Missing Soldiers Office in 1864, with the support of President Lincoln and a grant to provide information to families on the status of their missing soldiers. She rented rooms in DC, and by 1868 the office had replied to 41,000 of over 62,000 inquiries. Military ID tags were not standard issue, so through painstaking searches, interviews with soldiers, and in dialog with Dorrance Atwater, whose work at Andersonville Prison was to keep track of military headstones, the office was able to locate thousands of soldiers. Five years later, suffering from depression and PTSD and unable to locate more soldiers, Barton closed the Missing Soldiers Office in 1869 and left for Europe to seek her next venture, leaving letters and other items behind.

In 1996, a government worker named Richard Lyons was surveying a dilapidated building prior to demolition when he says he felt the touch of a hand. He turned and saw the corner of an envelope hanging from an attic crawl space. Climbing a ladder to see what it was, he discovered over 200 boxes of letters and artifacts, including a sign that read *Missing Soldiers Office*. Clara Barton, who would go on to establish the American Red Cross, had sublet rooms on the third floor of that very building for an office and living quarters. The sign confirmed the treasure trove that Lyons had found.

After the 1911 Triangle Shirt Waist Factory fire in New York brought sweeping new fire safety regulations, the building, with no fire escapes, was boarded over to avoid the required upgrades, and hidden away for over 130 years, virtually still intact. Future owners only used the first floor for retail. That original Shaw letter remains in Clara's bedroom in what is today the Clara Barton Missing Soldiers Office Museum.

Address 437 7th Street NW, Washington, DC 20004, +1 (202) 824-0613, www.clarabartonmuseum.org | Getting there Metro to Gallery Pl–Chinatown (Red, Yellow, and Green Line); bus D6 to E and 7th Streets NW, bus 70, 74 to 7th and E Streets NW, or bus 80, P6 to Gallery Place | Hours Fri–Sat 11am–5pm | Tip The Shakespeare Theatre Company, considered by many to be the premier Shakespeare company outside of London, has two theaters nearby: the Lansburgh Theatre (450 7th Street NW, Washington, DC 20004, www.shakespearetheatre.org), and Sidney Harmon Hall (610 F Street NW, Washington, DC 20004, www.shakespearetheatre.org). Take in a show or a theater tour.

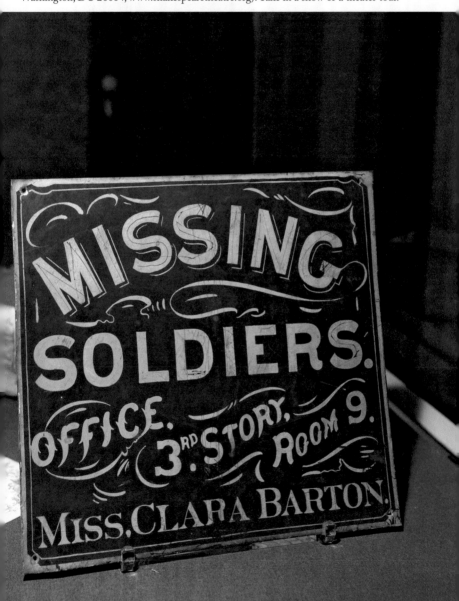

72 Mitsitam Café

It means, "Let's eat!"

Be sure to check out all the stations at the recently refreshed Mitsitam Native Foods Cafe at the Smithsonian's National Museum of the American Indian. Campfire Grill, Mitsitam Chef's Table, The Four Corners, and Woodlands & Coastlines stations offer dishes made from recipes and indigenous foods sourced from across the Americas, from northmost Canada to southernmost Argentina. Executive Chef Alexandra Strong and Sous Chef Toshiba Veney are the first all–female duo to lead the kitchen of a Smithsonian cafe and are carrying forth what their predecessors began.

Founding Chef Richard Hetzler established the café as a forerunner in the research and offering of Native dishes and wrote a cookbook showcasing its bounty. Then, Chef Freddie Bitsoie, Diné (Navajo), established an anthropological perspective for the food, encouraging every effort to research traditional recipes, ingredients, and their histories. Staying true to the traditions of the food is the key to the menus here. Food and storytelling go hand in hand in Native culture, whether the stories are about the food itself or told while cooking it.

Menus rotate each season, combining opposite seasons of the northern and southern hemispheres, which allows the serving of southern summer produce simultaneously with northern winter items, and vice versa. Special foods are served for festivals, fairs, and holidays that may be taking place in the museum or in the Americas, such as Day of the Dead and an annual Chocolate Festival.

"Mitsitam" means "Let's Eat" in the language of the Piscataway and Delaware people of this region. Among the staples here are planked salmon, bison burgers, and fry bread. Tribes have an ongoing discussion over whose fry bread recipe is best, and if you haven't tried it yet, start here. The stars of the menu are the uncommon and delicious seasonal dishes that keep locals coming back.

Address National Museum of the American Indian (NMAI), 4th Street SW and Independence Avenue SW, Washington, DC 20024, +1 (202) 633-1000, www.nmai.si.edu | Getting there Metro to L'Enfant Plaza (Green, Yellow, Blue, Orange, and Silver Line) or Smithsonian (Blue, Orange, and Silver Line); bus 32, 36 to Independence Avenue and 4th Street SW | Hours Café: daily 11am–4pm; Museum: daily 10am–5:30pm | Tip The highly symbolic sculpture Allies in War, Partners in Peace on the museum's 4th floor commemorates the friendship between the Oneida Nation and the United States forged during the American Revolution (www.oneidaindiannation.com/allies-in-war-partners-in-peace).

73 MLK Time Capsule
A skateboarder never notices

Every day, countless people congregate on Freedom Plaza, aptly renamed for Dr. Martin Luther King, Jr., with its square-block sized map of L'Enfant's city plan, and walk over a large, engraved stone on the west side of the plaza with the words "On this site is the Martin Luther King Jr. Holiday Commission Time Capsule…"

President Ronald Reagan signed a bill in 1983 making the third Monday of each January Martin Luther King, Jr. Day. On the second commemoration of MLK Jr. Day in 1987, Ebenezer Baptist Church, King's home church, was rededicated in Atlanta and Coretta Scott King announced the time capsule project. The capsule traveled to 110 cities around the country for a year so that people could contribute to its contents.

In 1988, Presidential Proclamation 5760 stated in part, "Martin Luther King's words were eloquent because they were borne not by his tongue alone but by his very being; not by his being alone but by the beings of every one of his fellow black Americans who felt the lash and the sting of bigotry; and not by the living alone but by every generation that had gone before him in the chains of slavery or separation…"

The capsule was buried on January 12, 1988, in a ceremony officiated by HUD Secretary Samuel Pierce, Jr. with Mrs. King, King's family, and friends. The capsule contains items from King's life that represent the man and his life's work. There is one of his bibles, a pastoral robe, photos, sermons, speeches, audio cassettes of his orations contributed by people who recorded them, a laser recording of his "I Have a Dream" speech, a miniature Liberty Bell inscribed with "Let Freedom Ring," and the Presidential Proclamation. DC Delegate Walter Fauntroy, a King confidant, added a 51-star flag that he hoped would be the flag of the United States, to include the District of Columbia, by the time the time capsule is opened in 2088.

Address Freedom Plaza, 14th Street, between Pennsylvania Avenue and E Street NW, western end near the fountain | **Getting there** Metro to Metro Center (Red, Blue, Orange, and Silver Line); bus 32, 33, 36 to Pennsylvania Avenue and 14th Street NW | **Hours** Unrestricted | **Tip** Old Post Office Tower offers panoramic views of the District, Maryland, and Virginia (1100 Pennsylvania Avenue NW, Washington, DC 20224, www.nps.gov/thingstodo/old-post-office-tower.htm).

74 Mount Zion Cemetery
A stop on the Underground Railroad

For about 40 years prior to the Civil War, the Underground Railroad was a dynamic and extremely clandestine network of abolitionists, anti-slavery activists, who risked life and personal liberty to transport enslaved people fleeing from bondage in the South to freedom in the northern US and Canada. There is little written documentation of the stops along the routes, for safety and illiteracy reasons, but oral histories offer insight into the operations and risks that abounded. Vocabulary of the railroad was used – "stations" were hiding places; "conductors," those who led enslaved people to freedom; "packages" or "cargo," the freedom seekers; while "station masters" offered shelter.

Just up from Rock Creek, which would have served as a watery pathway to keep bounty hunters and their sniffing dogs off the scent of an escapee, is a small vault where bodies were stored to await burial, mostly in winter, awaiting spring thaw. The vault, nestled into a slope of a hill, now accessible by a contemporary staircase, would have been secretly stocked with food, water, blankets, and clothing for the weary and terrified travelers running for their lives.

Stories tell of this vault being a hideaway for passengers on the Underground Railroad to stop during the day to eat and sleep until they could continue on their journey north under cover of night.

Congregants of the Mount Zion United Methodist Church down the street, and other local abolitionists and stakeholders, would have provided money and goods to stash inside the vault for those who needed them. Imagine having to seek hidden food and shelter among the icy cadavers.

How exactly travelers would have found this spot is not specifically known, but word of mouth and discreet symbols would have connected the stations along the routes. Mount Zion Church is one of the few organizations that kept any written records to document the activity of the Underground Railroad.

Address 2501 Mill Road NW, Washington, DC 20007 (behind Dumbarton House) |
Getting there Metro to Dupont Circle (Red Line), use Q Street exit, walk west on
Q Street NW, right on 27th Street NW to cemetery; bus D 2, D 6 to Q and 27th Streets NW |
Hours Unrestricted | Tip Dumbarton Oaks is home to a noteworthy Byzantine and pre-
Columbian art collection, and site of the Dumbarton Oaks Conference, where the United
Nations was born in 1944. Take a stroll through the lush gardens that are glorious in spring
and fall (1703 32nd Street NW, Washington, DC 20007, www.doaks.org).

75 __ Mumbo Sauce at Yum's
The foodstuff of urban legend

The stuff of Chinese carry-outs has found its place on the menus of trendy restaurants and bars, and yet it remains a staple of fried fast-food joints. Mumbo sauce is long considered DC's flavor, though it migrated here from its supposed origins in Chicago, to date an issue of some debate. By local accounts, the original DC mumbo sauce was invented at the now defunct Wings-n-Things carry-out in Shaw in the early 1960s, and apparently has never met its equal. Yum's II, a classic carry-out, comes close with its salty, crunchy chicken wings with a thick, slightly zippy sauce that makes for a great picnic lunch.

Though Washingtonians may argue, the credit for the invention of mumbo sauce probably goes to Argia B. Collins, Sr. a Mississippian who made his way north to Chicago in the Great Migration and opened a barbecue joint on the South Side, where he drenched his barbecue and fried foods in his ketchup-based sauce.

No two sauces are alike, and not everyone even agrees on how to spell it. It may be seen on menus as Mambo, Mumba, Mombo, Mumble, Mummbah, or any variation that gets the point across. This red sweet and savory sauce has a base of tomato concentrate, distilled white vinegar, and sugar. Other flavors like pineapple or orange juice, soy sauce, hot sauce, generally Tabasco, and ginger may be added. Ketchup is often used as the tomato base, giving a sweeter flavor to the mix. DC natives, particularly African Americans, are highly likely to have grown up with this flavor in neighborhood restaurants and on family tables. In his ode to the condiment, DC musician Christylez Bacon sings, what else but "Mambo Sauce."

Try a sampling and select your favorites. Here are a few more to try: the DC Bloody Mary at Perry's; chicken wings at The Hamilton at 600 14th Street NW; and the long-standing Wings and More Wings at 1839 Benning Road NE.

Address Yums II Carry-Out, 1413 14th Street NW, Washington, DC 20005, +1 (202) 232-5608 | Getting there Metro to U Street–African-Amer Civil War Memorial–Cardozo (Green and Yellow Line); bus 52, 54 to 14th and P Streets NW or G2 to P and 14th Streets NW | Hours Mon open 24 hours, Tue–Thu 11am–2:30am, Fri & Sat 11am–4am, Sun noon–midnight | Tip The nearby Mary McLeod Bethune Council House National Historic Site is the home of the tireless educator and civil rights activist. It also served as the headquarters of the National Council for Negro Women in the 1940s (1318 Vermont Avenue NW, Washington, DC 20005, www.nps.gov/mamc/index.htm).

76 New Hampshire Period Room

A children's attic playroom

The Daughters of the American Revolution Headquarters (DAR) is the largest building of its kind owned exclusively by women. DAR Headquarters includes the collections of the DAR Museum, DAR Library, and the Americana Collection. The ornate library is the second largest genealogy library in the country.

The DAR Museum preserves objects made and used prior to industrialization. DAR societies representing 31 states maintain period rooms that resemble rooms ranging from a 1690 "home office" to parlors, pubs, and living quarters from different decades of the 19th century. Of these rooms, the New Hampshire Period Room is particularly charming.

Set up as a 19th-century children's playroom, the New Hampshire Period Room reflects the changing attitudes towards childhood during that period. Instead of just small adults, childhood was recognized as a separate period of life with special needs. Playrooms began to be built as a separate room, although usually in attics or other distant parts of the house. It is a beautiful wood-paneled room, angled to match the rise of an attic roof, filled with children's furniture and toys as well as several dollhouses. One dollhouse seems to double as a chest of draws. An impromptu tea party is attended by several dolls, and a team of horses pulls a 19th-century passenger carriage.

A nearby credenza displays a Humpty Dumpty Circus exhibit with all of its animals and performers. This circus was introduced in 1903 by the A. Schoenhut Company, a manufacturer started in 1872 that built toy pianos and other instruments and later added dolls, dollhouses, and circus figures, of which the Humpty Dumpty Circus is one of the most popular and collectible.

A visit to this attic feels like walking into a life-size doll house.

Address Daughters of the American Revolution Headquarters, 1776 D Street NW, Washington, DC 20006, +1 (202) 628-1776, www.dar.org | Getting there Metro to Farragut West (Blue, Orange, and Silver Line) or Farragut North (Red Line); bus 33 to H and 17th Streets NW | Hours Mon–Fri 8:30am–4pm, Sat 9am–5pm | Tip American Red Cross National Headquarters offers free tours of its glorious building while teaching the noble history of the organization. Look for the splendid Louis Comfort Tiffany windows (430 17th Street NW, Washington, DC 20006, www.redcross.org/about-us/who-we-are/history).

77 Newton's Apple Tree
From the roots of science history

Amid a few dozen embassies, on the former grounds of the National Bureau of Standards (NBS), is planted an unassuming tree in a cozy park. The plaque under the tree, however, gives one pause. This apple tree is an actual progeny of the "Flower of Kent" tree that inspired Sir Isaac Newton's theory of gravity. Originally planted and raised by the US Department of Agriculture, an NBS scientist acquired 4 cuttings in 1957 and opted to plant one on the grounds of the Bureau in tribute to Newton, whose work impacts their daily business. In 2000, the DC tree succumbed and was replaced by a clone of the first. As the trees were cultivated from cuttings, rather than from seeds, which may be pollinated by any other random flora, this one is a genetic replica of Newton's tree in England. A second tree was planted on the new campus (now known as NIST) when they relocated to the Maryland suburbs.

As the story goes, Newton returned to his mother's home, Woolsthorpe Manor, in Lincolnshire, England after his university was closed in 1666 due to the Black Plague. It was here that he sat in the orchard contemplating the forces of nature that he had been studying. An apple fell from the tree before him, apparently not on his head, and that small observation begat the theory of gravity. Newton's famous tree was felled by a storm in 1820. Some stories say that was the end of the tree, but others have documented that it remained rooted and grew back strong and still lives in the British countryside, some 400 years old, and certified as one of Britain's 50 Great Trees.

It is unclear how cuttings were brought to the United States, but there are Newton trees at several eminent universities and institutions around the world, some clones and some from seeds. The DC tree continues to thrive under the watchful eye of its diplomatic neighbors and security forces.

Address 3500 block of International Drive NW, Washington, DC 20008 | Getting there Metro to Van Ness–UDC (Red Line); bus H2 to Van Ness Street and International Drive NW, or bus L2 to Connecticut Avenue and Van Ness Street NW | Hours Unrestricted | Tip The Levine School of Music is one of the country's preeminent community music education centers for all ages, and it's the only all-Steinway community school in the world. See website for concerts, recitals, master classes, and more (2801 Upton Street NW, Washington, DC 20008, www.levinemusic.org).

78__Oldest Mini-Golf Course
The most important shot in golf is the next one

Surrounded by the Washington Channel, East Potomac Park Golf Course, the Potomac River, and a tunnel of lush cherry trees is a delightfully charming miniature golf course. It is listed as the oldest continuously operating miniature golf course in the country, and has its place on the National Register of Historic Places.

As early as 1913, East Potomac Park was identified as a location for a golf course, in concordance with the McMillan Plan of 1901 to build "model public play grounds" throughout the city. This miniature course opened in the spring of 1931, 10 years after the adjacent 36-hole golf course, upon which President Harding was one of the first to play.

At the height of the Great Depression, there were some 50,000 mini-golf courses around the US that provided affordable family recreation. With the advent of extra sensory entertainment, the number of courses has decreased to about 4,000.

The simplicity of décor, what remains of the Garden Style of the 1920s and 30s, of this course may deceive players into thinking that it is a quick and easy playing game. Some of the layouts of original holes remain, each outlined with regional masonry flagstone and pebbled aggregate and covered in traditional bright-green AstroTurf. The miniatures of iconic DC buildings have vanished with restorations over generations, but a historic sign in the center of the course offers a glimpse back to the good old days.

What the course may lack in contemporary décor, it is not lacking at all in challenges and a great offering of nostalgia, with a water-generated cross breeze that will cool the player and possibly challenge a moving ball. This par-53 course is great fun for both children and for smack-talking adults, who should take note of one of the rules, "no competitive putting." Don't be fooled by hole 18. It might just test your putting skills!

Address 972 Ohio Drive SW, Washington, DC 20024, +1 (202) 554-7660, www.golfdc.com/miniature-golf | Getting there Metro to Smithsonian (Blue, Orange, and Silver Line), Independence Avenue exit, and walk about 1.4 miles; metro to Southwest Waterfront (Green Line), walk to the Wharf and take the free jitney across the channel (seasonal); Capital Bikeshare from any station to Hains Point/Buckeye and Ohio Drives SW, bike station 31273 | Hours See website | Tip Innovative ARTECHOUSE merges technology, colors, whimsy, and augmented reality into an interactive touch and motion activated sensory display. All ages welcome during the day, 21 and over in the evening (1238 Maryland Avenue SW, Washington, DC 20024, www.artechouse.com).

79 Omni Shoreham Ghost Suite

Apparition in residence

Not everyone, even long-time staff, believes in the ghost that purportedly haunts the Omni Shoreham Hotel since the 1930s. And like in the game of telephone, the stories and names vary in the telling.

Some have seen her late at night creating a scene in the hall outside room 870, now known as the Ghost Suite and consequently the priciest digs in the elegant Art Deco hotel that was one of the finest in the city when it opened in 1930. She might be Grace Doherty, wife of minority owner Henry Doherty, or the hotel's executive housekeeper, Juliette Brown, who lived in room 864 in the Dohertys' private suite and looked after their family. Some say it is their daughter Helen Doherty, though her obituary shows that she died at home in Denmark in 1964. Perhaps she teleports to Calvert Street.

One morning in the 1930s, Brown took ill, seemingly reached for the phone, perhaps to call for a doctor, and died abruptly without being able to place her call. Her body was eventually found after an engineer noticed the phone line off the hook and went to investigate. Several years later, Grace Doherty too died in the suite, also of presumed natural causes.

When Henry Doherty moved out in 1973, the vacant room became derelict, holey roof and all, until the hotel was renovated in 1999. Guests in adjacent rooms have complained of noises coming from the suite, and oddities, like moved objects, lights and TVs going on and off, and the feeling that someone had passed by when no one was there. Four in the morning, around the time that Juliette died that day, is the ghostliest hour.

Spend a night in the Presidential (Ghost) Suite, enjoy a classic cocktail in the Marquis Bar, or dine at Robert's Restaurant – and keep an eye open for the ghost!

Address 2500 Calvert Street NW, Washington, DC 20008, +1 (202) 234-0700, www.hauntedrooms.com/washington-dc | Getting there Metro to Woodley Park–National Zoo station (Red Line), or bus L 2, 96 to Connecticut Avenue and Calvert Street | Hours Lobby unrestricted; Reservations required to stay in the Ghost Suite. | Tip Commune with over 8,400 ancestors in Walter Pierce Park, once burial grounds where African American Civil War soldiers and sailors were buried alongside many involved in the 1848 failed slave escape aboard the schooner *Pearl*. Historic markers tell the story (Calvert at Biltmore Streets, Washington, DC 20009).

80__ Orphée Mural
Marc Chagall's mythical mosaic

Nestled in a grove of legacy redwood trees between Coosje von Brueggen and Claes Oldenburg's giant typewriter eraser and the café is the intricate and iridescent *Orphée*. Once located in a Georgetown backyard, this 17-foot-by-10-foot mosaic mural was transplanted to the National Gallery of Art Sculpture Garden by an elaborate feat of conservation and engineering.

While visiting his friends, art collectors Evelyn and John Nef, at their home in 1969, Marc Chagall declared the house "perfection" but thought that he should create something for the garden. He designed the 10-part work in his French atelier and hired Italian mosaicist Lino Melano, who had worked with Braque, Picasso, and Léger, to fashion it from Murano glass, Carrara marble, and Italian stone. The Nefs expected a small mosaic and were surprised by this magnificent piece. It was installed in 1971 in a tailored brick and steel wall in the garden. In 2009, Evelyn bequeathed the work to the National Gallery, which then embarked on the plan to relocate it. The production of cataloguing, dismantling, moving, and reinstalling the mosaic took a team of experts over three years to complete.

Chagall and Melano had carefully selected stones to absorb the light, and an untold number of glass pieces, tesserae, to reflect the light, which gives the mosaic different luminous qualities depending on the light of day and the weather. Chagall was known for his allegorical personages and here are the Greek mythological figures of Orpheus with his lute, Pegasus the winged horse, and the Three Graces. On the lower right is a couple resembling the Nefs, and in the left corner a group of immigrants waiting to come to America, reminiscent of Chagall's own odyssey of being smuggled out of Nazi-occupied France.

Visit this splendid work up close and from a distance at different times of day to enjoy its colors and shine.

Address Constitution Avenue and 9th Street NW, Washington, DC 20408, +1 (202) 216-9397, www.nga.gov/visit/sculpture-garden.html | Getting there Metro to Archives–Navy Memorial–Penn Quarter (Green and Yellow Line); bus 32, 36 to Pennsylvania Avenue & 7th Street NW; DC Circulator (National Mall Route) to Madison Drive and 7th Street NW | Hours Daily 10am–5pm | Tip The National Gallery of Art Sculpture Garden hosts a skating rink from mid-November to mid-March. Enjoy live jazz on many Friday evenings (Constitution Avenue and 9th Street NW, Washington, DC 20408, www.nga.gov/visit/ice-rink.html).

81___Owney
the Railway Mascot
The dog who traveled the world by mail transport

In 1888, a scruffy little dog turned up in the Albany, New York post office, seemingly attracted by the smell of the mailbags, and was allowed by postal workers to stay. He hung around the post office and eventually began riding the mail wagons across town to Union Station. And then came the trains. Before he set off on mail trains, postal workers gave him a leather collar with a tag that read, "Owney, Post Office, Albany, New York." They considered him a good luck charm, as no train that he traveled on ever derailed, blew up, or was robbed, all of which were hazards of the time. He was given medals and tags to show where he had been, and the Albany workers collected them whenever he returned. In 1894, the Postmaster General presented him with a vest for the heavy tags. The next year, he was sent as a goodwill ambassador on an around-the-world sailing voyage, bringing a brush, comb, and blanket in a tiny suitcase and shipped as a "Registered Dog Package." Stops included Mexico, Canada, Japan, China, Singapore, Suez, Algiers, and the Azores. In 9 years, he logged some 400 stops and over 140,000 miles on his travels.

Through the 1890s, Owney's celebrity grew. A reporter once wrote of his tags, "when he jogs along, they jingle like the bells on a junk wagon." By 1897, he was old and going blind. One day he stowed away on a train to Toledo, Ohio, where, during an interview with a reporter, he bit his handler. Soon after, he met his sad demise, shot by an unknown perpetrator. Albany postal workers chipped in for a taxidermist to have him preserved and sent him to the US Postal Service Headquarters in Washington, where he presided until 1911, when he was donated to the Smithsonian. When the National Postal Museum opened in 1993, Owney once again became the mascot of the mail train. Owney was honored in 2011 with his own "Forever" stamp.

Address National Postal Museum, 2 Massachusetts Avenue NE, Washington, DC 20002, +1 (202) 633-5555, www.postalmuseum.si.edu | Getting there Metro to Union Station (Red Line), walk across First Street NE | Hours Daily 10am–5:30pm | Tip On November 8, 1958, Harry Winston mailed the 45.52 carat Hope Diamond in a plain brown envelope to the Secretary of the Smithsonian Institution for $2.44 in postage. It was delivered safely to the National Museum of Natural History. The envelope is in the collection of the National Postal Museum.

82 Perry's Drag Brunch

Hello, Gorgeous!

There is no entertainer quite like the Mistress of Ceremonies at Perry's Sunday Drag Brunch. Welcome to the longest-running drag brunch in town, playing in Adams Morgan since 1991. Perry's prides itself on its contemporary Japanese fare from their new, award-winning chef in this sophisticated venue. But on Sundays, it turns into a glorious, sequined whirlwind of dancing Queens.

Once you are seated, fill up your plate at the varied and very tasty brunch buffet because the next thing you know, the dining room gets overtaken with energy and laughter as the bawdy and hilarious MC India Larelle Houston takes the floor. "We have been cross dressing for Christ for over 30 years!" she exclaims during her raucous yet warm welcome. Bejeweled in a vibrant bounty of rhinestones and sequins, she gets the crowd going and reminds the audience that tips are welcome. "If you can, take a one, five, ten, twenty, hundred, and let it move you."

The more the audience responds, the more entertaining the repartee becomes. And then the lip-synching and showwomanship begins. The multi-ethnic troupe of well-seasoned and award-winning talents, accompanied by various generations of club music, sashay, strut, and shake their way among the tables. Whitney Gucci Goo began her career here and is known for doing high kicks and splits like a college cheerleader – but in stilettos. The performers, all veterans of the DC scene, rotate occasionally. Sofia Carrero has been performing here since 1991, and she's still got it!

The MC takes a pause midway to call for guests who are celebrating anything from birthdays to divorces and other milestones. She gives each person heartfelt affirmation and then invites them all to dance for tips as another club tune belts out. In a personal moment, India observes that the show's many layers of sexual, ethnic, and social representation are the reason for its enduring success.

Address 1811 Columbia Road NW, Washington, DC 20009, +1 (202)234-6218, www.perrysam.com/#Brunch, perrysdragbrunch@gmail.com | Getting there Metro to Woodley Park–Zoo/Adams Morgan (Red Line); bus 42, L2 to Columbia Road and Biltmore Street NW; DC Circulator (Woodley Park–Adams Morgan–McPherson Square Route) to Calvert Street and Columbia Road NW | Hours Sun Brunch 10am–noon & 1–3pm | Tip The Potter's House is a coffee house, bookshop, and gallery that "provides a place where neighbors can become friends, ask big questions, and build movements" (1658 Columbia Road NW, Washington, DC 20009, www.pottershousedc.org).

83 Peterbug Shoe Academy
Not your average cobbler shop

Peterbug Shoe Repair Academy, one of few remaining cobbler shops, doubles as a training school for those wishing to learn the trade. Its namesake, John "Peterbug" Matthews, is a beloved pillar and mentor of his neighborhood. Known to the kids as "Mr. Peterbug," he has been repairing and making shoes for nearly 50 years. His mission is to offer opportunity to learn a trade so that underserved people may become gainfully employed citizens.

He was a naughty child with a stutter, and his dad's punishment was to send him to a local cobbler to learn how to repair shoes. A school counselor told him to "go to vocational school because you are not college material." He not only went to vocational school but on to higher education and became a master craftsman. A mentor demonstrated the need to teach kids skills, social responsibility, and business acumen, wisdom he has paid forward through his academy since 1974. His Shoeber has kids with bicycles picking up shoes for repair and learning customer service skills.

He has survived urban blight, the crack epidemic, and gentrification, and his business continues to thrive. A giant grill, tethered to the side of the building, is lit for neighborhood events, including concerts on the small stage on the patio behind his building. He hosts Peterbug Day, an annual block party held May or June, including a 5k Fun Run.

The city named the 400 block of 13th Street SE "Peterbug Way." He was shocked and honored, and he quipped, "Don't you need to be dead for two years first?" Recently, Mr Peterbug has also launched a mobile shoe repair bus in which he offers demos in schools and repairs shoes for seniors citizens at practically no charge. His shop has been designated a historical DC landmark. Every community should be blessed with an inspirational and hilarious leader like Mr. Peterbug.

Address 1320 E Street SE, Washington, DC 20003, +1 (202) 689-4549, www.peterbugshoeacademy.com | **Getting there** Metro to Potomac Avenue (Blue, Orange, and Silver Line); bus 32, 36, to Pennsylvania Avenue and 13th Street SE | **Hours** Call for hours | **Tip** The Philadelphia-style pretzels at The Pretzel Bakery are made fresh daily and may be eaten solo, in 3 flavors with house-made dips, or in the form of breakfast pretzel sliders, bombs, dogs, or calzones (257 15th Street SE, Washington, DC 20003, www.thepretzelbakery.com).

84 Planet Word Privies

Flush with bathroom humor

Do your spelling bee prep or a foreign language lesson while you heed the call of nature in one of the restrooms at Planet Word, DC's new language arts museum. Each restroom is embellished with words, phrases, synonyms, and euphemisms for toilets, the act of using them, and what comes out. In converting the historic, Adolf Cluss-designed Franklin School into a museum, every wall had to be utilized. Inspired in part by old school graffitied bathrooms, even the walls and stalls in the restrooms humorously reflect the theme of exhibits on each floor.

Euphemisms for the action of using the restroom decorate the first floor. "A visit to the oval office," so apropos in DC, sadly was only offered up by a visitor after the museum was completed and thus only exists in story. On the second floor, in tandem with the library there, the walls are covered in puns, with notable nods to Shakespeare and Descartes. On the third floor, you can learn to say, "Where is the bathroom?" in a bounty of languages, per the theme of the floor's gallery about the diversity of the world's languages (plus, it's a "necessary" phrase no matter where you go).

Should you attend an event on the fourth floor, you'll find synonyms for "bathroom" in other languages, with a QR code to identify each one. Museum founder Ann Friedman tells of a contractor who didn't recognize the Mongolian word for "bathroom" written in Cyrillic on one tile. He inadvertently placed it upside down. See if you can spot the now upright tile. On the mezzanine, in an area unfortunately limited to the public, the custom-made tiles designed specifically for these walls depict animals, even dinos, and the scat (or is it coprolite?) that they drop.

So when you need to rest on the porcelain throne, engage in the omnipresent vocabulary lessons of this fun and playful museum. With more stalls, ladies can enjoy more content.

Address 925 13th Street NW, Washington, DC 20005 (entrance on K Street), +1 (202) 543-0539, www.planetwordmuseum.org | Getting there Metro to McPherson Square (Blue, Orange, and Silver Line) or Farragut North (Red Line), or bus 80, D 4, D 6, S 2, S 9, X 2 to K and 13th Streets NW | Hours Mon, Wed – Fri 10am – 5pm, Sat & Sun 10am – 6pm | Tip Speaking of words, the *Star Spangled Banner* was first sung at the notable Brown's Marble Hotel in 1814 at what is now an office building (601 Pennsylvania Avenue NW), where a plaque commemorates the occasion.

85 Prairie Dogs

Cutest zoo animals, and natives too

There is hardly a more entertaining or engaging group of animals in the National Zoo than the black-tailed prairie dogs. This species of ground squirrels, named "dogs" due to their bark that signals alarm, have been in residence at the zoo since its creation.

In 1887, prairie dogs were brought from the West by William Temple Hornaday, along with 14 other North American species, to live on the National Mall behind the Castle, now the Enid A. Haupt Garden, where they lived until 1891. Hornaday, Chief Taxidermist at the Smithsonian Institution, who in 1887 became the first head of the Department of Living Animals, took a trip to the West where he was shocked by the noticeable disappearance of millions of American bison that once roamed in herds of thousands. He began a campaign to save the animals that were in danger of extinction. Hornaday's vision and determination were instrumental in the development of the Smithsonian National Zoo, established by an Act of Congress and "dedicated to the advancement of science and the instruction and recreation of the people," along with the Conservation Biology Institute, which launched the Conservation Movement.

The father of landscape architecture, Frederick Law Olmsted was commissioned to design a new zoo facility in a section of Rock Creek Park, where it remains since it opened in 1891. The zoo is a world leader in global animal conservation and breeding programs.

Prairie dogs, an umbrella species, are little threatened in the wild and contribute greatly to grassland ecosystems. Their burrowed towns host many other species too. These funny, burrowing, talkative animals, unlike some of the better-known residents of the National Zoo, command an audience with their antics. There is great pleasure in sitting on the ledge around their habitat and watching them dig, scout, bark, and scuttle about.

Address National Zoo, 3001 Connecticut Avenue NW, Washington, DC 20008, +1 (202) 633-1000, www.nationalzoo.si.edu, info@si.edu | Getting there Metro to Woodley Park–Zoo/Adams Morgan (Red Line); bus L2 to zoo entrance, or bus 96 to Connecticut Avenue and Calvert Street NW | Hours Daily, summer 8am–6pm; winter 8am–4pm, free time-stamp tickets required | Tip Visit the other legacy zoo animals, Lucy and Gally, two youngest American bison to become members of the zoo family. Of the 6 species that were original residents, the collection no longer has American foxes, badgers or lynxes, but wild deer can be found throughout Rock Creek Park just outside the zoo.

86 — The President's Walk
The failed assassination of President Reagan

Still known to locals as the "Hinckley Hilton," the venerable Washington Hilton Hotel has the largest ballroom in town and hosts events at which the US president is the guest of honor. On March 30, 1981, President Ronald Reagan had just given a speech to members of a trade union, marking the 100th visit by a sitting president to the hotel. He was ushered through the President's Walk, a tunnel built during the hotel's construction two years after the Kennedy assassination. It looks like a garage entrance that connects to the ballroom and is still used by VIPs for security and to avoid crowds both inside the hotel and out.

The president was waving to onlookers as he walked to his awaiting limousine. Six shots were fired from close range, injuring the president, two police officers, and Press Secretary James Brady, who had been shot in the head. The shooter, John Hinckley, who had inserted himself into the crowd of reporters and photographers, was quickly identified and slammed up against the wall by police officers as the president's limo sped off towards the White House. It was only in transit that the officer in the car realized that the president was bleeding. Even Reagan himself was not yet aware that he had been shot. The limousine changed course for George Washington Hospital.

The always good-humored President Reagan survived and had some choice comments during his ordeal. A few days after the emergency, surgeon Joe Giordano recounted his conversation with the president just prior to surgery, who had commented "Please tell me you are all Republicans," to which Giordano replied, "We're all Republicans today." When he awoke from surgery to a nurse holding his hand, Reagan asked her, "Does Nancy know about us?" Moments later his wife arrived, and in his disarming way, he quoted defeated boxer Joe Dempsey, saying, "Honey, I forgot to duck!"

Address Washington Hilton Hotel, 1919 Connecticut Avenue NW, Washington, DC 20009, +1 (202) 483-3000, www.historichotels.org/hotels-resorts/washington-hilton/history.php | **Getting there** Metro to Dupont Circle (Red Line), use Q Street exit and walk four blocks north on Connecticut Avenue NW; bus 42, L 2 to Connecticut and Florida Avenues NW | **Hours** Unrestricted | **Tip** Fleet Feet, a legacy small business owned by the parents of a former DC mayor, will hook you up with your next pair of comfy walking shoes (1841 Columbia Road NW, Washington, DC 20009, www.fleetfeetdc.com).

87 — Riggs Bank Building
Money launderers to the dictators of the world

Built in 1836 in Classical Revival style, the former Riggs National Bank building is just across from the Treasury Department and steps from the White House. William Corcoran built it as a brokerage house, and it evolved into the bank where twenty-three presidents kept their money. Until its demise in 2003, Riggs called itself "the most important bank in the most important city in the world."

As the bank grew in the 20th century, it catered to embassies, diplomats, and national governments. It became the personal bank to infamously brutal dictators of Chile and Equatorial Guinea. Executives of the bank sought out these men to open accounts and involved themselves in offshore money transfers, intake of large amounts of cash, and innumerable forms of money laundering of the ill-gotten gains of men who were taking from their countries' coffers and accepting bribes from corporations. There are stories of Chilean Embassy operatives walking into the bank with paper grocery bags full of cash to deposit in the accounts of its dictator and of a man bringing in briefcases full of bills for an African strongman.

The Justice Department fined Riggs $25 million, the largest bank fine ever, for money laundering for foreign dictators and embassies. Riggs was fined another $16 million for violating the US Bank Secrecy Act. The once eminent bank crumbled under the pressure of investigations into years of money laundering and scandal and was sold to PNC Bank in 2003.

The building is a designated historic landmark. In its early days, the bank was the financier of William Morse's Telegraph Machine, Admiral Peary's first expedition to the North Pole, the Mexican-American War, the 1860s expansion of the US Capitol building, and the purchase of Alaska. It has now become the Milken Center for Advancing the American Dream, ironically owned by a convicted and later pardoned felon.

Address 1503 Pennsylvania Avenue NW, Washington, DC 20005 | Getting there Metro to Metro Center (Red, Blue, Orange, and Silver Line), use 13th Street exit; bus 32, 33, 36 to 15th and G Streets NW | Hours Unrestricted from outside only | Tip Visit the nearby Inter-American Development Bank's Staff Cultural Center Gallery (1300 New York Avenue NW, Washington, DC 20577, www.iadb.org/en/knowledge-resources/creativity-and-culture/exhibitions) featuring Latin American and Caribbean artists, from IDB member countries. Check the website for openings, virtual events, and concerts.

88 Ripley Center Mural

Illusions of an ancient city

The image of an ancient, excavated, and partially crumbled promenade with Roman looking details opens up to the Arts and Industry Building in the foreground and the Castle up on the left. Two sphinxes post sentry at the entrance, while the bull heads, decapitated statues, and grotesques stationed on the walls look over the pathway. It appears to be a sunny day, and the shadows play over the painted brick walkway. And none of it is real, except for the potted plants to the sides that provide depth of field for the painted greenery that hangs from above.

This two-story-tall trompe l'oeil mural appears as if you could walk right into it. An alluring work of wall art, it is underground on the National Mall below the Castle and the Enid A. Haupt Garden. The copper-topped pagoda between the Smithsonian Castle and the Freer Gallery is the entryway to this often overlooked art space on the bottom floor of the S. Dillon Ripley Center.

If you cup your hands to the side of your eyes to eliminate peripheral vision, it makes the 3D effect even more real as you walk towards the wall. Trompe l'oeil, which literally means "deceives the eye," is an ancient painting technique that makes objects on a flat surface look three-dimensional – optical illusions, if you will.

In conversation, muralist Richard Haas referred to this particular mural as an 18th-century perspective of a neo-Roman city that became Washington, or an "excavationesque" site that reveals the new Smithsonian buildings above.

Natural light from skylights three stories above makes this underground space feel airy and provides for realistic illumination of the scene. As the area is fairly quiet, it is easy to imagine yourself walking down the promenade and up towards the colorful and enticing Victorian and Renaissance Revival architecture of the Arts and Industry Building and the neo-Gothic Castle.

Address 1100 Jefferson Drive SW, Washington DC 20560, +1 (202) 633-1000, www.si.edu/museums/ripley-center, info@si.edu | Getting there Metro to Smithsonian (Blue, Orange, and Silver Line); bus 52 to Independence Avenue and 12th Street SW | Hours Daily 10am–5:30pm | Tip Smithsonian Nighttime Adventures for ages 8–12 are offered periodically at the National Museum of Natural History (Constitution Avenue & 10th Street NW). Children and a chaperone enjoy after-hours activities and adventures among the treasures www.smithsonianassociates.org/nights).

89 Rock Creek Park Horse Center

Riding in the middle of the city

If you love all things horse, then the Rock Creek Park Horse Center is a mecca for experienced and budding equestrians alike. Rock Creek Park has always had an association with horses, and the authorization act establishing the park called for the creation of bridle paths as soon as possible. In the early years, the paths served as carriage roads for stables and horse owners outside the park. Fox hunts and equestrian exhibitions were popular as well. In 1958, the Horse Center was established, and since 1972, it has been located on Glover Road in the park.

The Horse Center takes full advantage of the 13 miles of bridle path within the park, and serves as the starting point for rides.

The Horse Center offers a full slate of services. Owners can board their horses in the box-stall stables. Group and individual riding lessons are available year round. Barn Days combine group riding and horse care lessons with arts and crafts. Spring break and summer camps introduce kids to horses and riding. Holidays bring special activities for children, like Pumpkin Pony Rides – costumes encouraged – and Reindeer Rides. Among the more innovative activities at the Horse Center is therapeutic riding instruction, where teachers work with clients to address emotional and psychological issues and physical rehabilitation. One famous client of the program was James Brady, former White House Press Secretary, who was injured in the attempted assassination of President Reagan in 1981.

Visit the website for public events and class schedules and updates. By taking advantage of the many trails throughout the park, riders have a beautiful way to escape urban life and see the seasons change up close. Watching the fall foliage and reconnecting with nature as you ride a horse along a bridle path is an almost Zen experience. Just reserve your ride well ahead of time!

Address 5100 Glover Road NW, Washington DC 20015, +1 (202) 362-0117, www.rockcreekhorsecenter.com, horsecenter@guestservices.com | Getting there Metro to Friendship Heights (Red Line) and transfer to bus E4 to Military and Glover Roads NW, walk 0.2 miles along Western Ridge Trail or Glover Road to the Horse Center | Hours See website for activities and events | Tip Bring a picnic and find a beautiful piece of grass near the Horse Center or the Visitors Center, or walk along Glover Road to one of the nearby picnic groves to take in the sounds, scents, and scenery. No alcohol is allowed in Rock Creek Park.

90 __ Rock Creek Planetarium
Night sky in the park

Mrs. Seymour, the fondly named giant projector in the center of the planetarium, beams to life, and so begins your exploration of the cosmos. A National Park Ranger is the narrator, science teacher, and occasional comic relief. The shows are created to show the sky from the perspective of the planetarium, located on the northern end of 1,754-acre Rock Creek Park, just off one of the cross-park thoroughfares. Built in 1960, this is the only planetarium in the entire National Park System, made even more unusual by its location in the heart of an urban park.

Ranger Tony is the creator of the planetarium programs that are geared for all ages. The show "Young Planetarium" teaches small children about the solar system; "Seasonal Night Sky" offers a look at the current season's alignment of stars and planets for ages 5 and up; and "Exploring the Universe" tells of the science of astronomy and showcases several notable cosmologists and physicists whose work has brought us our current understanding of the universe. Colored with the ranger's stories and telling of Native American legends and audience participation, particularly from the children, the shows become educational entertainment for all. Each month, the rangers offer a specialty show that may range from African skies for Black History Month to Thanksgiving skies.

For 60 years, the National Capital Astronomers and the NPS have been setting up telescopes in the field near the Nature Center and Planetarium to allow beginner stargazers and devotees the chance to enjoy their passion for exploration. Telescopes are set up in the field just west of the planetarium one Saturday a month, from April through November, and all are welcome.

As ranger Jeff notes, the planetarium offers a way to appreciate the night sky from Rock Creek Park, as there is no camping allowed in the park.

Address 5200 Glover Road NW, Washington, DC 20015, +1 (202) 895-6070,
www.nps.gov/rocr/planyourvisit/planetarium.htm | **Getting there** Metro to Friendship
Heights (Red Line) and transfer to bus E 4 to Military and Glover Roads NW, walk
0.2 miles along Western Ridge Trail or Glover Road to Planetarium | **Hours** See website for
program schedule | **Tip** Fort DeRussey is one of the remnants of the ring of 68 forts that
surrounded the city during the Civil War, and noted for having kept the Confederates at
bay during the short but fraught Battle of Fort Stevens (Western Ridge Trail, Washington,
DC 20012, www.nps.gov/places/fort-derussy.htm).

91 Scottish Rite Temple

Of Freemasons and the city

Scottish Rite is a branch of Freemasonry, a complex fraternal organization dating back centuries to the trade guilds of England. Historically, guilds were segregated and very tradition bound. George Washington, Benjamin Franklin, and John Hancock were Freemasons, along with about a third of the Continental Army officers of the 1700s.

Flush with cash in 1911, the Scottish Rite of Freemasonry Supreme Council, 33rd Degree chose 16th Street, the meridian of the city, as the site of their new headquarters. Uncommon tales abound here.

During construction of the building, special dispensation was given to build railroad tracks to bring the tons of stone columns from Union Station to the site. A painting of George Washington being sworn in as the first president in New York hangs in the dining room. He has his hand on a Masonic bible procured last moment at a nearby lodge when the original bible was forgotten elsewhere. It is said that the non-denominational bible best reflected his desire to show no religious preference.

Here is the first library ever open to the public. In the mid-1900s, the librarian invented a unique cataloguing system – it is not your Dewey Decimal – for 250,000 volumes that represent a body of knowledge, chiefly Masonic history, now often used for genealogical research. They hold 700 to 800 periodicals, including copies of some European ones that were lost during World War II when Hitler targeted Freemasons for assisting Jews. A complete collection of Scottish poet Robert Burns' works was donated by a benefactor.

In the American Room, affectionately known as "The Room of Interesting Tchotchkes," is the flag that Buzz Aldrin, a Freemason, took to the moon in 1969. It is noted with great pride that "we are the only ones besides the US government who can say that we flew a flag on the moon."

1733

Address 1733 16th Street NW, Washington, DC 20009, +1 (202) 232-3579, www.scottishrite.org, council@scottishrite.org | Getting there Metro to Dupont Circle (Red Line) and walk seven blocks northeast; bus S2 to 16th and S Streets NW | Hours See website for tour schedule | Tip For some more over-the-top Art Deco Masonic architecture, walk up the street to the DC Scottish Rite headquarters (2800 16th Street NW, Washington, DC 20009, www.dcsr.org).

92 Shakespeare's First Folios

The Bard's work on Capitol Hill

There is no imagining contemporary theater or high-school English classes without Shakespeare's fellow thespians John Heminges and Henry Condell, who did the world the boundless favor in 1623 of publishing *Mr. William Shakespeare's Comedies, Histories, and Tragedies*, or, *The First Folio*. You might assume that most of the folios are in England. In fact, they are on Capitol Hill.

In college, Henry Folger was inspired by an 1864 Ralph Waldo Emerson speech in which he declared that Shakespeare's "moral sentiment" was more suitable to the youthful US than to the Old World from where he came. In the early to mid-1900s, when English families were liquidating vast estates, Henry and his wife Emily began collecting Shakespeare works in earnest. Folger set his focus on the *First Folio* collection, the first printed editions of Shakespeare works, seeking out folios with imperfections that he felt had personality, and over the years amassed 82 of the 235 known surviving copies, of only 750 believed to have been printed. This is more than any other library in the world. It was a first in 1623 that a large format book, normally reserved for royal proclamations, history, and theology, compiled the works of a single author grouped by comedies, histories, and tragedies.

The 400-year-old tomes are now exhibited in a new, state-of-the-art gallery, where they may all be seen together for the first time. The pages of one folio will be turned regularly so as to appreciate the size of the manuscripts and the consequence of their content. The title page portrait by Martin Droeshout is one of only two known accurate Shakespeare images. 18 of the 36 works selected by Heminge and Condell were never published in the Bard's lifetime including *Macbeth*, *Twelfth Night*, *Julius Caesar*, *Comedy of Errors*, *Taming of the Shrew*, and *All's Well That Ends Well*. The library has just reopened after an extensive renovation to best showcase the Bard's works.

Address 201 East Capitol Street SE, Washington, DC 20003, +1 (202) 544-4600, www.folger.edu | Getting there Metro to Capitol South (Orange, Blue, and Silver Line) or Union Station (Red Line); bus 32, 36 or DC Circulator (Union Station–Navy Yard Route) to Pennsylvania Avenue and 2nd or 3rd Streets SE | Hours Sun 11am–6pm, Tue & Wed 11am–6pm, Thu–Sat 11am–9pm, extended evening hours on performance days | Tip The renowned and newly renovated Folger Theatre, designed as a composite of theater styles of the Jacobean era (1567–1625), is home to both traditional and innovative productions of the works of Shakespeare and many other playwrights (201 E Capitol Street SE, Washington, DC 20003, www.folger.edu/folger-theatre).

93 __ The Shoe Room

We are the shoes. We are the last witnesses.

The stale smell of the ages pervades the small room. They are displayed in a stark white space, with a walkway that takes you through this pool of shoes, separated by only a low glass barrier on either side. Stylish pretty ones. Utilitarian ones. Those of the working class and the elite. Adult's and children's. The occasional colorful one stands out from the majority of brown and black leather.

The source of this vast collection of human belongings is Majdanek, a forced labor camp near Lublin, Poland, where Jews and non-Jews were brought with the intention that they would work to maintain the Ostindustrie GMBH, the Nazi network of manufacturing plants. The shoes were to be repaired and redistributed to German workers. Majdanek was the first concentration camp to be liberated in 1944 by the Soviets, and as it had been quickly abandoned, it was found virtually intact. Soviet soldiers photographed mounds of shoes among the possessions stolen from victims at Majdanek and other camps and killing centers. Periodically, the museum collects the shoes and sends them back to the State Museum of Majdanek so that they may be treated, preserved, and rotated to other museums around the world. Meanwhile, a new shipment of shoes arrives for display, and this labor of love and remembrance is perpetuated.

In an adjacent shielded exhibit is a photo of a bin of human hair. This remnant of the wholesale desecration and sale of human bodies and spirits, shaved from the heads of victims and used as stuffing for furniture, industrial felt, and yarn for socks for Nazi submariners and railway conductors, is sacrosanct, perhaps never to be physically displayed here.

A 101-year-old woman, who sat at the survivor's desk each Sunday, said, "This is not a story. It is my experience." Another survivor stated, "There are days when even I, who lived the Holocaust, can't believe it happened."

Address United States Holocaust Memorial Museum, 100 Raoul Wallenberg Place SW, Washington, DC 20024, +1 (202) 488-0400, www.ushmm.org | Getting there Metro to Smithsonian (Blue, Orange, and Silver Line), Independence Avenue SW exit; bus 52 to Independence Avenue and 14th Street SW | Hours Daily 10am–5:30pm. Free tickets required, book online. | Tip At sunset, stroll over to the National Mall nearby to indulge in the evening glow of the Smithsonian Castle, Enid Haupt Garden, and the US Capitol. The photo opps are stellar (National Mall, Washington, DC 20560).

94 Shop Made in DC
Bringing local makers to the fore

An exciting, artful, and edible venture has become a star of the retail scene in DC. Shop Made in DC is a private/public collaboration that has brightened up the handmade and small business landscape. The brainchild of co-owner Stacey Price, these inviting stores are designed to be "vibrant ecosystems," where handcrafters, appreciative shoppers, and food lovers come together with small business development in a community of creativity.

In a city full of makers, Shop Made in DC is dedicated to representing artists, crafters, and food and beverage purveyors, whose products are designed, crafted, and made entirely in the District. There are now over 200 makers and 5,000 products in the inventory. The driving idea is that offering an outlet for makers to bring what they sell to a broader marketplace also helps grow the neighborhood economy and community. The shops, along with a network of DC small businesses, art agencies, and non-profits, promotes the success of makers and their passion projects. Shop Made in DC continuously layers in the work of new makers, who can apply online to participate.

Whether you're shopping for a "gift to me, from me," or a gift for someone else, you will find a colorful and varied selection of everything from stationery to apparel; jewelry to edibles; décor to lotions and potions; and ceramics to accessories. Every maker is certified "Made in DC," and each display features a sign that gives a brief intro of the maker, their products, concept, and inspiration. It is through these stories that shoppers can identify with the people behind the products.

There are now shops in The Wharf, Georgetown, Union Market, Scott Circle, and Capitol Hill. The one at the Wharf is usually the most bustling. Workshops and maker events are a regular occurrence at the larger shops and a fun way to meet crafty neighbors and do some making of your own.

Address The Wharf, 10 District Square SW, Washington, DC 20024, +1 (202) 270-1529, www.shopmadeindc.com, see website for other locations | Getting there Metro to L'Enfant Plaza (Blue, Orange, Silver, Green, and Yellow Line) or to SW Waterfront (Green Line), or bus 52 to Maine Avenue and 9th Street SW | Hours The Wharf, Mon–Thu 10am–8pm, Fri–Sun 10am–9pm; see website for other store hours | Tip Just down from Shop Made in DC at The Wharf is a historic marker commemorating the 1848 Pearl Incident, in which 77 enslaved people boarded the *Pearl* schooner in a failed attempt to escape enslavement (embedded in the ground at Wharf & 7th Streets SW).

95 Smokey Bear's Office

Only you can prevent forest fires

Smokey Bear is the iconic symbol of forest fire prevention, and one of the most successful communications campaigns ever. Smokey has his office in the US Forest Service Visitors Center, where he greets friends in a warm, automated baritone, as he reclines with his feet propped up on his desk. Take a photo with him, or rest inside the log cabin and watch videos about the work of the USFS. Children can take home souvenirs of Smokey and Woodsy, the anti-pollution owl, for free.

In 1944, Japan launched thousands of 33-foot, handmade paper incendiary balloons carrying fragment bombs across the brisk Pacific airstream, with the intent to start forest fires in North America, in the diabolical Operation Fugo. A US scientist figured out the mysterious "jellyfish in the sky" after many were spotted, and some detonated in the Pacific Northwest. With that, a national forest fire awareness campaign was launched. It began with the 1943 poster, "Our Carelessness, Their Secret Weapon." In 1947, the now renowned slogan, "Remember – Only YOU Can Prevent Forest Fires," was launched with an image of a bear wearing jeans and a US Forest Service hat, pouring water on a fire. Today the slogan still resonates.

Found clinging to a tree after a massive 1950 fire in New Mexico's Lincoln Forest was a 3-month-old black bear cub. "Hotfoot Teddy" was nursed back to health. The Forest Service seized the chance to make the cub a living corollary to the original campaign.

Amidst great fanfare, and renamed Smokey, he arrived at the National Zoo to become one of the most famous and beloved residents. He died in 1976, leaving an adopted heir, Little Smokey, also from Lincoln Forest. Smokey was eulogized in *The Washington Post*. Uniformed rangers took his body back to Lincoln Forest, where he is memorialized with a plaque, not far from where he had been found 26 years earlier.

Address USDA US Forest Service Visitors and Information Center, 1400 Independence Avenue SW, Washington, DC 20250, +1 (202) 832-1355, www.fs.usda.gov/about-agency/forest-service-headquarters | Getting there Metro to Smithsonian (Blue, Orange, and Silver Line), Independence Avenue SW exit; bus 52 to Independence Avenue and 14th Street SW | Hours Mon–Fri 8:30am–4:30pm | Tip Octagon House was built by one of the largest slave owners in Virginia. Used as the interim White House during the War of 1812, it is allegedly very, very haunted (1799 New York Avenue, Washington, DC 20006, www.architectsfoundation.org/octagon-museum).

96 — The Spice Suite
There is no fun in selling bottles of fennel

This petite apothecary of spices is an adventurous cook's playground and an in-a-rut cook's inspiration, where magical spice mixes can be obtained to cure culinary doldrums or to stimulate taste buds. There are no single flavor spice jars here.

The proprietor, Angel Gregorio, a former school principal, describes it as a perfume counter. "There are no rules. If you love it, you use it on what you love. You can get excited by smelling." She is an avid wanderer, and all of her travels include spice shopping in places known only to locals. Her habit is to get in a taxi and tell the driver, "take me someplace where tourists don't go." It is on these adventures that she procures the flavors of the places she visits, which in turn are made into the imaginative flavors of her mixes. She generally starts with spices and a scent that inspire her to cook at that moment, from there a flavor palate and a meal are built. Each week she creates a new spice blend, a flavor of infused bourbon and infused honey, also available as a kit. Richly infused olive oils and balsamic vinegars on tap change periodically.

The key to this sensory trip around the world is to consider that "food is like fashion, and you should mix what is unlikely." Once a month, shoppers may mix their own spices at the bar.

The Spice Suite playlist, with its broad array of sound, entices you to tap your toes as you shop.

Regular and rotating vendors, known as The Spice Girls, run the shop and sell their handmade goods in exchange for giving Angel the days off to create and travel in pursuit of fresh spices. Her uncommon mixes of flavors are the essence of this delightful shop. The store has recently moved to become the anchor of Angel's new endeavor Black + Forth, an architecturally enticing micro-mall in which Black entrepreneurs are incubating and growing their own small businesses.

Address 2201 Channing Street NE, Washington, DC 20018, +1 (202) 506-3436, www.thespicesuite.com, thespicesuite@gmail.com | Getting there Metro to Rhode Island Avenue (Red Line), transfer to bus 86 towards Calverton to Rhode Island Avenue & 20th Street NE, and walk about 10 minutes SE to Channing Street | Hours See website for hours | Tip Visit the nearby District Clay Center to learn how to make vessels in which to serve those spiced up dishes you will be cooking with your new spices (2414 Douglas Street NE, Washington, DC 20018, www. districtclaycenter.com).

97 — Theodore Roosevelt Island

A living memorial with a rich history

Theodore Roosevelt Island is a living tribute to the 26th US President and the man who created the national park system. A granite-paved plaza on this 88-acre island in the middle of the Potomac River is centered by a statue of Roosevelt and several tablets engraved with quotations from his writings. But the island has a varied history spanning several centuries.

George Mason, a Founding Father of the United States, purchased the island in 1724. At the time, it was called Analostan Island, and it became a prosperous cotton and corn estate. Following George Mason's death, his son John built a summer residence famous for its gardens and social activities. Several US presidents and the King of France all visited the island. The Masons vacated in 1831 when debts piled up and a causeway made the Potomac River stagnant. By 1861, the island passed into the hands of the former mayor and postmaster of Washington.

In 1863, following the Emancipation Proclamation that freed "all persons held as slaves," the island became Camp Greene, the training grounds and residence for some 700 men of the 1st United States Colored Troops (USCT). Their presence on the island was kept a secret to prevent racially motivated violence by surrounding secessionists. Between 1863 and the end of the war, the 1st USCT saw action in both Virginia and North Carolina.

In the 1930s, the ruins of the Mason mansion were removed – only a historical plaque remains – and the island was transferred to the Federal Government for the creation of a memorial to President Roosevelt. The famous landscape architect Frederick Law Olmstead Jr. directed the restoration of the original woodland and the planting of 20,000 native trees. Today, ecological zones of forest, swamp, and tidal marsh along with two miles of open trails celebrate Teddy Roosevelt, the man known as the "Great Conservationist."

Address George Washington Parkway at Key Bridge, www.nps.gov/this/index.htm |
Getting there Metro to Rosslyn (Blue, Orange, and Silver Line) then walk 0.6 miles north
on North Lynn Street to the Mount Vernon Trail, then south to the pedestrian bridge |
Hours Daily 6am–10pm | Tip *Washington Post* reporter Bob Woodward met his top-secret
informant "Deep Throat," now known to be former FBI Associate Director Mark Felt, six
times in 1972 and 1973 in a parking garage across Key Bridge from Georgetown. Look for
the historic signpost that marks the spot (1816 North Nash Street, Rosslyn, VA 22209).

98 Thomas Jefferson Papers
To be perused up close

Thomas Jefferson's inexhaustible collection of letters, documents, diaries, and notes are a source of bountiful insight into his life and that of the emerging nation. In the elegant lobby of the Jefferson Hotel, a mere five blocks from the White House, the hotel's private collection of eight documents from his storied life are hanging on the wall adjacent to the reception desk.

Lawyer Edward Bennet Williams, a former owner of the hotel, is said to have amassed this collection as a lot at auction, including them in the sale of the hotel in 2005. The letters and documents are dated from 1743 to 1826, spanning Jefferson's tenure as Governor of Virginia to Secretary of State to President.

Of note is a personal check written by President Jefferson to his faithful coachman, Joseph Dougherty, in the amount of $13.10 ½ to pay his salary. It is countersigned by Jefferson's banker, John Barnes, to show that the check is good for its value. It is signed "your very humble servant," a typical sign off in his personal letters and documents. Fascinating is the elegant and legible handwriting of the man.

Others include an old boilerplate, tri-lingual international trade document allowing the transport of lumber from the port of New Orleans, a French holding and not yet part of the US, to New York, then a Dutch colony. Spanish is the third language, as St Augustine was under Spanish rule and not yet part of the US. A ship's charter, its "passport," is stamped with a seal to show legitimacy, bears an elaborate drawing of a ship and scalloped edges, perhaps to match up to a second document of authenticity. As Secretary of State, it was the job to be the chief administrative officer of the land, handle correspondence to foreign governments, write on behalf of the president, and be the keeper of record. It is in this job that Jefferson amassed many of these documents.

Address 1200 16th Street NW, Washington, DC 20036, +1 (202) 448-2300, www.jeffersondc.com/about-us/history-renovation | **Getting there** Metro to Farragut North (Red Line) or McPherson Square (Blue, Orange, and Silver Line) use L Street exit; bus S2, S9 to 16th Street and M Street NW | **Tip** The Metropolitan AME Church is known as the national cathedral of African Methodism. Formed by freed and enslaved people in 1821, it has been at the forefront of advocacy for abolitionism, civil rights, religious freedom, and AIDS education (1518 M Street NW, Washington, DC 20005, www.metropolitaname.org).

99__Transportation Walk

Round, round, get around, I get around

The US Department of Transportation Building may look like any other government office, but pump those brakes! You have ambled right into a 7-block-long timeline of US land, water, space, and air transportation history. In keeping with the notion that sidewalks promote walking, the Walking Museum of Transportation encircles the buildings.

It is divided into four eras, each with a timeline on the surface of a building: Encounter and Exploration 1600–1811; Industry and Expansion 1812–1899; Greater Mobility 1900–1946; and Modern Era 1947–present. Read about innovators, some of note, and some unknown, and visually trace their inventions through time.

The bikes are meant to be climbed on, the ship wheels to be turned, and the brightly colored, vintage gas pumps to be handled. Airplanes, from Wright Flyer to modern jets, fly on poles overhead. The large fountain flows in warm weather with several different metal ships seemingly traversing it along the horizon. Gateway bridges hang overhead and frame the walk, each a different architectural style being traversed by cars, trains, wagons, trucks, and bikes. Small triangular "It happened right here" signs instruct you to look up at the airport flight path, or pause to note that the metro is beneath your feet.

There are models of all different forms of transport. Milestones in transportation history are a reminder of how much our modes of travel have evolved since Columbus' caravels, Conestoga wagons, and the Wright Brothers' airplanes. Trailblazers are honored for their contributions to how we have managed to get around, and models of some of their inventions are there on which to be played.

As the architect notes, everything is interactive, indestructible, and meant to be touched so you can see how it works. The intent is that neighbors and visitors will play in the park while learning a few historical tidbits.

Address 100 Tingey Street SE, Washington, DC 20003, www.capitolriverfront.org/go/
walking-museum-of-transportation | **Getting there** Metro to Navy Yard-Ballpark (Green
Line); bus P 6, V4 to M Street and New Jersey Avenue SE | **Hours** Unrestricted | **Tip**
Ice Cream Jubilee owner Victoria Lai says that her ice cream "is my way to bring joy to
others through imaginative flavors and irrepressible smiles." And that she does, with small
batches of dairy products from happy cows living a mere hour away (301 Water Street SE,
Washington, DC 20003, www.icecreamjubilee.com).

100 __ Tricycle House
Riding up the wall

One of the bonuses of home ownership is the opportunity to express one's style, interests, and passions through architecture and design. This can explain why house tours are popular in cities throughout the United States. One house in the Mount Pleasant neighborhood has been attracting curious glances and closer inspection for many years.

The Tricycle House at 1726 Park Road NW is one half of a pair of complementing, semi-detached duplex houses on a block comprised of several twin structures. Of late, current renters have amplified the outside of the house itself with decorations that truly make it sparkle, particularly for holidays, cherry blossom season, and LGBTQ-related events, which make for some glorious photos.

1726 Park Road was designed originally by Nicholas R. Grimm, a prolific Washington architect who created over 1,200 buildings, including hundreds of row houses and flats. It was built in 1909 by one of the District's best-known builders and bankers of the period, Lewis E. Breuninger. In addition to Mount Pleasant, Breuninger helped develop several other residential neighborhoods including Park View, Colonial Village, Shepherd Park, and rows of houses in Columbia Heights with large front porches that were considered innovative at the time.

The current owners have used aptly known Tricycle House as a canvas to express their personal style and a considerable whimsy. The house's brick is painted yellow, and bright complementary colors trim the roof, window frames, and the underside of its wraparound porch. In the middle of the front yard is a tall sculpture, or a "trike tree," constructed of several red tricycles. Another bright red tricycle rides up the front of the house to an upper floor. And a yellow crayon scrawls a line across the right side of the house. Certainly, it is one of the most distinctive and fun residences in the city, and well worth the visit to Mount Pleasant.

Address 1726 Park Road NW, Washington, DC 20010 | **Getting there** Bus H 4 to Park Road and Mount Pleasant Street NW, or bus S 2, S 9 to 16th Street and Park Road NW | **Hours** Unrestricted from outside only | **Tip** Suns Cinema and Bar is a neighborhood spot that shows a variety of movies, mostly indie and classics (3107 Mount Pleasant Street NW, Washington, DC 20010, www.sunscinema.com).

101 _ True Reformer Hall

Duke Ellington's first paid gig

American music legend Edward "Duke" Ellington is widely known for playing big band jazz at the Cotton Club in Harlem. But he was born in Washington, DC in 1899 and went on to have a noteworthy music career there before moving to New York City at the age of 24. Growing up in Shaw, he and his family lived in six homes, none of which are protected as historical landmarks. Four of the houses are still privately owned and viewable from the outside. His birth home at 2129 Ward Place NW is now the site of a post office.

True Reformer Hall on U Street is one building that remains an important landmark in Ellington's legacy because it is here where he played his first paid gig. The building opened in 1903 as a structure that would "reflect credit upon the Negro race," according to the Reverend William Lee Taylor at the building's inauguration. It was designed, financed, and built by African Americans.

The True Reformers themselves were a benevolent organization founded to support the African-American community. Their building became an anchor of the U Street Corridor and Black Broadway, attracting more businesses and nightlife to the area. It housed the first black National Guard unit, on the lower floors. Upstairs were the ballrooms where Ellington and his first band, The Duke's Serenaders, played late into the evening. They earned 75 cents, or roughly $15 at current value.

Today, the most prominent tributes to Duke Ellington in DC are the Duke Ellington Bridge over Rock Creek Park, and the Duke Ellington School of the Arts in Georgetown. The school is a living memorial to the great musician, graduating prominent performers including Denyce Graves, Meshell Ndegeocello, and Dave Chappelle. You can still find many of the places where Duke Ellington lived, played, and made music, but True Reformer Hall is a place where he first made music history.

Address 1200 U Street NW, Washington, DC 20009 | Getting there Metro to U Street/
African-Amer Civil War Memorial/Cardozo (Green and Yellow Line); bus 90, 92, 96 to
Vermont and Florida Avenue NW | Hours Unrestricted from outside only | Tip Tagging
has turned from simple graffiti to striking street art. A tagging crew has been granted wall
space in the alley between Ben's Chili Bowl and Ben's Next Door (1211–1213 U Street NW,
Washington, DC 20009) where they periodically update their pulsating work.

102 Turkish Ambassador's Home

From bottle caps to jazz tradition

Edward H. Everett, innovative industrialist, known for inventing the crimped bottle cap for Coca-Cola bottles, hired architect George Oakley Totten, Jr. in 1914 to build this opulent mansion. Totten had come to Washington after a turn in Turkey to design the US Embassy and as architect to members of the court of the Sultanate of the Ottoman Empire. He fused some Turkish and European design elements into his architecture, which, fortuitously, melded well with its future occupants.

Second Turkish Ambassador to the US, Mehmet Münir Ertegün, was the first diplomat to occupy the residence, rented for his use in 1932. The Republic of Turkey bought the mansion in 1936, fully furnished. Middle son, Ahmet, first heard the Duke Ellington Orchestra as a child in London, which forever impacted him. Older brother Nesuhi would take him to hear live music and explain it. As a teenager living in DC at the height of racial segregation, Ahmet frequented the jazz clubs on Black Broadway, and the Howard Theatre in particular. He befriended many musicians and aficionados. He and Nesuhi began inviting musicians to the residence to jam for friends and colleagues. Nesuhi said in 1979, "You can't imagine how segregated Washington was at that time. Blacks and whites couldn't sit together in most places. So, we put on concerts… Jazz was our weapon for social action." Once the ambassador was asked in a letter from a senator why there were so many black people coming and going from the front door of his home and he replied, "Our friends enter through the front door, and should you ever come by, we will gladly let you in the back door."

Ahmet went on to co-found Atlantic Records and helped create the Rock and Roll Hall of Fame, into which he and Nesuhi were both inducted. Nesuhi founded Jazz Man and WEA International labels.

Address 1606 23rd Street NW, Washington, DC 20008 | Getting there Metro to Dupont Circle (Red Line); bus D2, D6 to Q and 23rd Streets NW, or bus N2, N4, N6 to Massachusetts and Florida Avenues NW | Hours Unrestricted from outside only | Tip Turkey continues their tradition of contributing to the culture of the country in which they serve by partnering with Washingtonian Jerome Barry, creator of The Embassy Series, the mission of which is to unite people of different cultures through musical diplomacy (www.embassyseries.org).

103___Uline Arena

The Beatles played their first US concert here

Beatlemania barreled into DC on February 11, 1964 on the tail of a smashing success on the Ed Sullivan Show two days prior. The Beatles played their first live US concert at the Washington Coliseum (aka Uline Arena) for a crazed crowd of 8,000. Harry Lynn, owner of the venue, was asked if he was interested in hosting the Beatles. He had never heard of them, but said yes. With one ad in the paper the concert sold out, generating enough revenue for Lynn to buy his wife a new convertible.

A snowstorm had grounded planes, so the press joined the Fab Four on a raucous train ride from New York to DC. The Beatles had races in the aisles, climbed into luggage racks, and served drinks in waiter uniforms. Paul later recalled taking the train through the snow. He said they had promised themselves not to play the US until they had a number one hit in the charts, so with "I want to hold your hand" at #1, they set off to conquer the Americas.

The Beatles performed a 35-minute, 12-song set. "Roll over Beethoven" started off the show, not planned, but it felt right. McCartney later said, "In retrospect, I should be telling [that] it was a calculated move to show the world of classical music that it was time they rolled over and made way for the delightful young sound that's going to take over." To maximize ticket sales, the concert was set up in a boxing ring, so the band had to rotate every few songs, with Ringo moving his drum kit each time. All the while they were enthusiastically pelted with jellybeans, after John had said jokingly how much he liked them. They never again played in the round. The sound of screaming was so loud that it nearly drowned out the concert.

Next to the customer service desk is the concert corner with seats, amps, and replicas of show posters as reminders of the epic performances that once graced this venue, now an REI flagship store.

Address REI, 201 M Street NE, Washington, DC 20002, +1 (202) 543-2040, www.rei.com/
stores/washington-dc | Getting there Metro to NoMa–Gallaudet U–New York Ave
(Red Line); bus 90, 92 to Florida Avenue and 2nd or 3rd Street NE | Hours Mon–Fri
10am–9pm, Sat 10m–8pm, Sun 10am–7pm | Tip Speaking of beetles, visit the Orkin
Insect Zoo at the National Museum of American History to weigh yourself on the
insect scale and flirt with butterflies in the Butterfly Pavilion (1000 Madison Drive NW,
Washington, DC 20560, www.si.edu/exhibitions).

104 Union Station Sentries

What are they hiding behind those shields?

Each day, thousands of commuters and visitors blaze a trail through the Main Hall of Union Station and fail to notice its architectural glory. Architect Daniel Burnham, chief designer of the Columbian World Expo of 1893, created Union Station as part of the 1901 McMillan Plan to beautify the city and elaborate the original Charles L'Enfant plan. 46 Roman legionnaire statues stand sentry over the Great Hall, part of Burnham's Roman bath-inspired Beaux Arts architecture. Sculptor Louis St. Gaudens submitted plaster models of the statues to the B&O and Pennsylvania Railway officials in 1906.

The officials were scandalized that many of the statues were nude or in tunic skirts, customary for Roman legionnaires, and they simply could not have genitalia on display for gentle lady travelers to see. After much dialog and compromise, St. Gaudens suggested that he place a large shield, held by the right hand of each statue, to obscure their lower half. The railway officials approved.

As with other athletic statues, there was a model for these sentries – California college student Helmus Andrews – who years later noted how unimpressed he was with them. All of the sentries were crafted and placed by 1913, six years after the station opened. St. Gaudens was paid $52,044.10 ($1.3 million today) for these and a series of six exterior stone sculptures, *The Progress of Railroading*, representing elements of railroad travel: fire, electricity, freedom, imagination, agriculture, and mechanics.

In his history of the station, author George Olszewski wrote, "As the Roman legionnaire symbolizes the far flung reaches of the Roman Empire, so these figures symbolize the far-flung ribbon of steel of the vast network of the American railroads reaching every part of the United States."

For a view behind the shields, the balcony of Pizzeria Uno offers an eye-level perspective.

Address 50 Massachusetts Avenue NE, Washington, DC 20002, +1 (202) 289-1908, www.unionstationdc.com | **Getting there** Metro to Union Station (Red Line); bus 96, D 6 to Massachusetts Avenue and 1st NE | **Hours** Unrestricted | **Tip** Named for Alice Paul and Alva Belmont of the National Woman's Party (NWP), the Belmont-Paul Woman's Equality National Monument is a tribute to the suffragettes and their work for women's voting and civil rights (144 Constitution Avenue NE, Washington, DC 20002, www.nps.gov/bepa/index.htm).

105__ The Uptown Theater
An art deco movie palace

"It's an invasion!" was the sentiment of residents in this cozy residential neighborhood the week that *Star Wars* opened in May 1977. The movie, inspired by George Lucas' love of Flash Gordon, was not expected to be even a minor success and opened in only 32 cinemas nationwide, including the Uptown Theater. Thanks to an ebullient review in *The Washington Post*, in which Gary Arnold gushed of Lucas, "He is in superlative command of his own movie-nurtured fantasy life," it garnered the attention of enthusiastic moviegoers who lined up for the first and month of subsequent showings to fill the palatial theater. The lines wrapped around the block, patrons picnicked on neighborhood yards, and all along the narrow streets drivers hunted for precious parking. The atmosphere was social and frenetic.

The Uptown Theater is the Grand Dame of the first-run movie houses that were built throughout the city from the 1920s to 1950s during the Golden Age of Cinema. Designed by architect John Zink, master of art deco and art modérne theaters, its grandeur is a standout along the Cleveland Park streetscape. This picture playhouse was opened by Warner Brothers in October 1936 during the Great Depression amid much fanfare. *Cain and Mabel*, starring Marion Davies and Clark Gable, filled the 2-story, 1,364-seat theater, appointed with velvet seats, the latest in projection and sound technology, climate control, and the largest screen in the city. When movies premiered, ornate fanfare flowed onto the sidewalks. Months-long runs in the 1950s and 1960s, refurbished classics, and world premieres have graced this 70mm Cinemascope screen, now with 840 stadium seats. The theater was named a historical landmark in 2022.

During the height of segregation, African-American patrons were not allowed to sit among white patrons in the orchestra and were relegated to the balcony. As luck would have it, those are the best seats in the house. The Uptown is currently seeking new owners.

Address 3426 Connecticut Avenue NW, Washington, DC 20008, +1(202) 966-5401 |
Getting there Metro to Cleveland Park (Red Line); bus L2, H2 to Connecticut Avenue
and Ordway Street NW | Hours Currently viewable from the outside only | Tip Walk west
on Newark Street NW, lined with elegant Queen Anne, gingerbread-style houses. Keep
your eyes open for Little Free Libraries, resembling colorful oversized birdhouses, where you
can leave or take a book for free.

106__ USNO Master Clock
Where accuracy really matters

We may use time to our advantage, or squander it. The passage of time is often taken for granted. So, if you need to reset your analog clocks, go see the Master Clock display just outside the US Naval Observatory (USNO).

The USNO Master Clock, in tandem with the Alternate Master Clock in Colorado, is the official timekeeper for the Department of Defense, Global Positioning System (GPS), and Standard Time for the United States. From time ball, to telegraph, to photographic zenith tube, to atomic resonance, the measure of time has become so accurate that now there is a clock that will not lose a second for 15 billion years.

Here is a quick lesson: Universal Time Coordinated (UTC), formerly Greenwich Mean Time (GMT), or Zulu Time, is a coordinated time scale kept by BIPM in France. A "master clock" is a precision clock that provides timing signals to "slave clocks" as part of a clock network. The International System of Units defines a second as "the time it takes a caesium-133 atom in a precisely defined state to oscillate exactly 9,192,631,770 times." Akin to the pendulum of a grandfather clock, the oscillation of an atom is far faster and stable than grandad's pendulum, and thus keeps the most accurate time measurable. Your GPS is based on the triangulation of the location of 4 out of 24 orbiting US satellites. Think about that the next time you yell at your phone.

The scientist guides for tours of the US Naval Observatory will break down the details of time into comprehensible nuggets of information on a subject that is integral to every single thing we do, every single day. Accuracy of time affects all forms of transportation and navigation, which affects everything from package deliveries to rocket launches.

Imagine the cumulative chaos that would ensue from the smallest inaccuracy. And speaking of time, email three months ahead to make tour reservations.

Address 3450 Massachusetts Avenue NW, Washington, DC 20392, +1 (202) 462-1767, www.cnmoc.usff.navy.mil | Getting there Bus N 2, N 4, N 6 to Massachusetts Avenue and Observatory Circle NW | Hours Unrestricted from outside | Tip The stunning, acoustically perfect Embassy of Finland across the street is incorporated into the surrounding woods and occasionally hosts public concerts and events (3301 Massachusetts Avenue NW, Washington, DC 20008, www.facebook.com/FinlandinUSA).

107 — Vace Italian Deli
Family recipes for the best pasta and pizza

"Have you ever gotten a piece of pizza to eat while you drive? I love that. It's good to take small bites and really enjoy it. Try one day, you will see," chuckles Blanca Calcagno, who co-founded Vace Italian Deli with her husband Valerio in 1976 and now runs the business with her daughter, Diana.

Valerio was a restaurant chef who always wanted his own pasta shop. He created recipes based in his Genoese family tradition, and the pair opened their tiny pasta shop in Cleveland Park, adding pizza to the menu after they were able to rent a space a few doors down for a pizza oven. The flagship is still in Cleveland Park, and today their pasta is made in their kitchen in Maryland, and pizzas are made on site in two locations.

Nearly edible smells wafting from the kitchen will have you wanting to try everything on the menu. Take home a pizza right out of the oven; handmade pastas and sauces; deli meats and cheeses; and other edibles, along with specialty items from Italy. The *agnolotti* and pizzas are amazing. Many of the employees have worked here for over 30 years, making pasta and pizza from scratch each day. Ask any of them behind the counter, including Manuel, who ran around the store in his diapers as a child while his Mom made pasta, what is their favorite item on the menu, and each has a different answer. Simply put, that means that you must try it all and choose your own favorite.

"From our family to yours," is the mantra of the Calcagnos. Neighbors who have eaten here forever now bring in their grandchildren for pizza and pasta, a tradition that makes Blanca happy. She invites visitors to come in to chat, whether hungry or not. Guaranteed, though, you won't walk out without some food in hand.

There are no seats, so you can take your carry-out food up the block to the public picnic tables, if you can make it that far without taking a bite.

Address 3315 Connecticut Avenue NW, Washington, DC 20008, +1 (202) 363-1999, www.vaceitaliandeli.com | **Getting there** Metro to Cleveland Park (Red Line); bus L2 to Connecticut Avenue and Macomb Street NW | **Hours** Mon–Sat 10am–8pm, Sun 10am–5pm | **Tip** For saucy, creative, and uncommon gifts and events, Femme Fatale DC is the place to go. The colorful, community-decorated shop is filled with handmade and vintage items made and curated by womxn. The staff is delightful and creative themselves (3409 Connecticut Avenue NW, Washington, DC 20008, www.femmefataledc.com).

108 Waldseemüller Map
Birth certificate of the Americas

Phillip D. Burden, a leading British map dealer and expert in cartography of the Americas, received a call in 1998 from another dealer with an urgent request to authenticate a map for a potential client. Under shroud of confidentiality, in a bank vault in Germany, he verified that A Map of the World According to the Traditions of Ptolemy and the Voyages of Amerigo Vespucci and Others, known simply as Universalis Cosmographia, was the only known surviving copy of the Martin Waldseemüller map of 1507.

This map is commonly accepted as the first to identify the continent of America and a distinct western hemisphere. The 34-square-foot 12-panel map, block printed on rag paper, was a feat of evolving innovation in printing as well.

Count Johannes Waldburg-Wolfegg's family owned the map for over 350 years. Father Joseph Fisher, teacher of history and geography, asked for and was granted access in 1901 to the family archives in the Wolfegg Castle in Baden-Württemberg, Germany, where he found this and three other maps, and published his findings. The US Library of Congress (LOC) was offered the map in 1912, but the price was too great. In 1992, as part of the 500th anniversary of Columbus' first voyage to the New World, the map went on exhibit at the National Gallery of Art. The US sent a letter of inquiry to the new Count Waldburg-Wolfegg, but German Chancellor Helmut Kohl denied the request for an export license of any item on the National Register of Protected German Cultural Property.

So it was not until a change in German leadership and that 1998 phone call that the talks progressed. The original client opted out, but the count succeeded in getting an export license. LOC spent four years raising $10 million, half of which luckily came via an obscure congressional allocation. The birth certificate of America now has its place of honor in the LOC.

Address US Library of Congress, Thomas Jefferson Building, 10 First Street SE, Washington, DC 20540, +1 (202) 707-8000, www.loc.gov/visit, vso@loc.gov | Getting there Metro to Capital South (Blue, Orange, and Silver Line) or Union Station (Red Line); bus 32, 36 to Independence Avenue and 1st Street SE | Hours Tue–Sat 10am–5pm | Tip Try the Senate Bean Soup, dating back to the early 1900s, available in most of the 11 eateries in Russell, Dirksen, and Hart Senate Office Buildings (Constitution Avenue between 1st and 2nd Streets NE, Washington, DC 20002, www.aoc.gov/senate/restaurants).

109 The Willard Lobby

So much history, and that's just in the lobby

In 1862, author Nathaniel Hawthorne wrote, "The Willard Hotel could more justly be called the center of Washington than either the Capitol or the White House or the State Department." In 1847, the Willard brothers leased the small hotel and gradually bought out the surrounding block of buildings. In 1904, it was reimagined and became DC's first skyscraper.

Through the 1800s, the hotel hosted many watershed and unusual events. Senator Henry Clay taught the bartender how to make a Kentucky Mint Julep, now the signature drink. Hungover congressman Philemon Herbert, upset for not being served a full breakfast after hours, got into a fight with the headwaiter and shot him. Sometimes a ghost, perhaps the headwaiter, appears in the Willard Room. President-elect Lincoln snuck into the hotel, disguised as a very tall woman, for fear of encountering conspiring Confederates. He left without paying his tab and later signed his first presidential paycheck over to the hotel. First Lady Julia Grant did not allow President Ulysses Grant to smoke cigars in the White House, so each day he would walk to the Willard to sip a brandy and smoke a cigar.

The University Club, National Press Club, and League of Nations were all formed here. Authors Mark Twain, Walt Whitman, Nathaniel Hawthorne, and Julia Ward Howe wrote in and about the hotel and Martin Luther King, Jr. tweaked his "I have a dream" speech before delivering it on the steps of the Lincoln Memorial. Each spring Milly the Duck returns and lays eggs in a courtyard planter and enjoys the fountain. After the ducklings hatch and grow some, the flock gets a Secret Service motorcade ride to the Reflecting Pool on the National Mall where they live until she returns again to the fountain.

Look up and find your state seal in the vaulted lobby ceiling and take a stroll or have tea in Peacock Alley, "promenade of the great and near great."

Address 1401 Pennsylvania Avenue NW, Washington, DC 20004, +1 (202) 628-9100, www.washington.intercontinental.com/history | Getting there Metro to Metro Center (Red, Blue, Orange, and Silver Line), use 13th Street exit; bus 32, 33, 36 to 15th and F Streets NW | Hours Lobby unrestricted; Round Robin Bar: Sun–Thu 4pm–midnight, Fri & Sat 1pm–midnight | Tip The tiny hotel museum at the F Street entrance showcases the glorious history through vintage documents and images of this grand dame, the first skyscraper in DC. Ask at the Uniformed Services desk (aka bell stand) about a short tour around the lobby. A gratuity is much appreciated.

110 Wright Flyer to the Moon

First in flight, first to the moon

"Dear Sirs: …I am an enthusiast, but not a crank in the sense that I have some pet theories as to the proper construction of a flying machine. I wish to avail myself of all that is already known and then if possible add my mite to help on the future worker who will attain final success. Yours Truly, Wilbur Wright" (May 30, 1899).

Wilbur Wright wrote this letter to the Smithsonian Institution on letterhead from the Wright Cycle Company in Dayton, Ohio, the little bike shop where he and his brother Orville had been experimenting with flying machines. On December 17, 1903, Orville Wright piloted the first controlled flight of a powered aircraft: 120 feet in 12 seconds. By the fourth flight of the day, Wilbur stayed aloft for 59 seconds and flew 852 feet.

The rest is aviation history, which, of course, you can see today at the National Air and Space Museum (NASM). The "Wright Brothers and The Invention of the Aerial Age" exhibit is dominated by the original Wright Flyer, even more light and elegant today than on that windy day in 1903. But there's one extremely poignant yet exceedingly unassuming artifact that you must certainly not overlook.

While preparing for his role as mission commander of Apollo 11, the first manned moon landing, Ohio native Neil Armstrong carried a fragment of wood from the Wright Flyer's left propeller and fabric from the upper left wing, both removed at Kitty Hawk after the fourth flight, in the Eagle lunar module. Look for the actual fabric and wood in a plaque at the exhibit exit, along with letters of authentication from the Orville Wright Estate and Commander Armstrong.

Everyone knows about the giant leap for mankind taken by Armstrong and Buzz Aldrin on July 20, 1969 on the surface of the moon. But very few people know about this emotionally and historically symbolic voyage from a bicycle shop to Tranquility Base, a journey of merely 66 years.

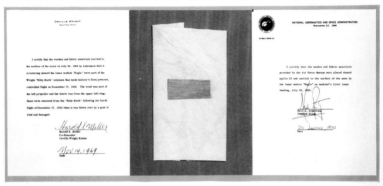

FIRST MANNED LUNAR LANDING

KITTYHAWK TO TRANQUILITY BASE

Address 600 Independence Avenue SW, Washington, DC 20560, +1 (202) 633-2214, www.airandspace.si.edu | Getting there Metro to L'Enfant Plaza (Blue, Green, Orange, Silver, and Yellow Line); bus 32, 36, P6 to Independence Avenue and 4th Street SW | Hours Daily 10am–5:30pm | Tip Take a 2,000-foot walk through our solar system, from the sun to each planet with the Voyage Project, a 1:1 billion scale model (Jefferson Drive SW, from 4th Street to the Smithsonian Castle, Washington, DC 20024, www.voyagesolarsystem.org).

111__Zero Milestone

All roads lead from Washington

You would be forgiven if you placed your bag or water bottle on top of this small stone post to take a picture of the south side of the White House, the National Christmas Tree nearby, or the Washington Monument to the south. It is only 2 feet square by 4 feet tall, and it's not hard to miss at the north end of the Ellipse. But if you did not take note of the Zero Milestone and brass plate nearby, you would miss the opportunity to experience a bit of American transportation history.

The Good Roads Movement pushed for the construction of better roads across the United States in the late 19th and early 20th centuries. The Zero Milestone was conceived by Good Roads Movement advocate Dr. S. M. Johnson in 1919 with the idea that all highways in the US and the western hemisphere should have a beginning point modeled after ancient Rome's Golden Milestone. Until today, all roads and distances in Washington and the surrounding suburbs are measured from it.

On July 7, 1919, the temporary marker for the Zero Milestone was dedicated during ceremonies launching the first of two military convoys that drove across the country to the West Coast. Then-US Army Captain Dwight D. Eisenhower was among the participants in the first convoy, and while all returned from the 3,000-mile trip convinced of the need to do something about the nation's roads, Eisenhower actually did do something about it. As president, Eisenhower credited his convoy experience as a motivating factor behind the establishment of the Interstate Highway System.

The permanent Zero Milestone was presented to the nation by Mr. Johnson in 1923 at a ceremony attended by President Warren Harding. The Zero Milestone is embellished with a bronze disc compass on its top and is engraved on its sides with the description of its purpose and to commemorate the two military convoys.

Address E Street, between 15th and 17th Streets NW, Washington, DC 20050, on the north side of the Ellipse, directly across from the White House south lawn | Getting there Metro to Metro Center (Blue, Orange, Red, and Silver Line) or Federal Triangle (Blue, Orange, and Silver Line); bus 32, 33, 36 to Pennsylvania Avenue and 14th Street NW | Hours Unrestricted | Tip After a few lightning strikes and finally the death of the National Christmas Tree, a tree from around the US is placed adjacent to the Milestone each year. The first National Christmas Tree was decorated on this spot by President Calvin Coolidge on Christmas Eve 1923 (www.thenationaltree.org/visit-the-tree-2/event-history).

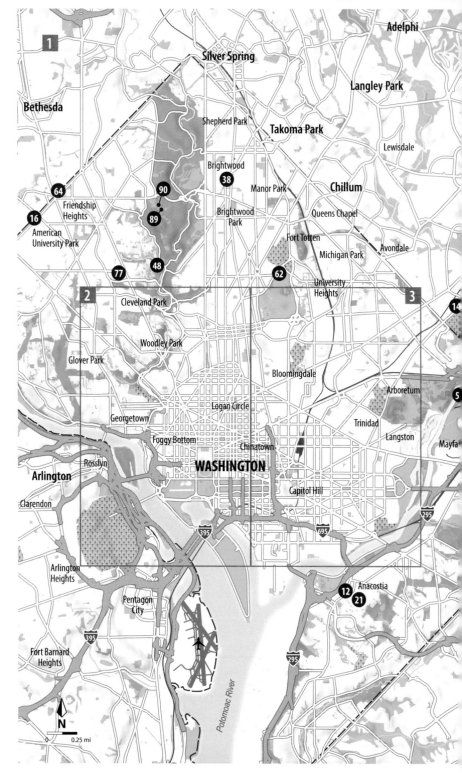

Lauri Williamson, David Wardrick
**111 Places in Black Culture in
Washington, DC That You Must
Not Miss**
ISBN 978-3-7408-2003-9

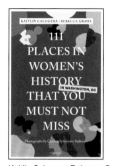

Kaitlin Calogera, Rebecca Grawl,
Cynthia Schiavetto Staliunas
**111 Places in Women's
History in Washington
That You Must Not Miss**
ISBN 978-3-7408-1590-5

Allison Robicelli, John Dean
**111 Places in Baltimore
That You Must Not Miss**
ISBN 978-3-7408-0158-8

Kim Windyka, Heather Kapplow,
Alyssa Wood
**111 Places in Boston
That You Must Not Miss**
ISBN 978-3-7408-2056-5

Jo-Anne Elikann, Susan Lusk
**111 Places in New York
That You Must Not Miss**
ISBN 978-3-7408-2400-6

Evan Levy, Rachel Mazor,
Joost Heijmenberg
**111 Places for Kids in New York
That You Must Not Miss**
ISBN 978-3-7408-1993-4

Wendy Lubovich, Ed Lefkowicz
**111 Museums in New York
That You Must Not Miss**
ISBN 978-3-7408-2374-0

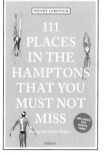

Wendy Lubovich, Jean Hodgens
**111 Places in the Hamptons
That You Must Not Miss**
ISBN 978-3-7408-1891-3

Brandon Schultz, Lucy Baber
**111 Places in Philadelphia
That You Must Not Miss**
ISBN 978-3-7408-1376-5

Amy Bizzarri, Susie Inverso
**111 Places in Chicago
That You Must Not Miss**
ISBN 978-3-7408-1030-6

Amy Bizzarri, Susie Inverso
**111 Places for Kids in Chicago
That You Must Not Miss**
ISBN 978-3-7408-0599-9

Michelle Madden, Janet McMillan
**111 Places in Milwaukee
That You Must Not Miss**
ISBN 978-3-7408-1643-8

Sandra Gurvis, Mitch Geiser
**111 Places in Columbus
That You Must Not Miss**
ISBN 978-3-7408-0600-2

Travis Swann Taylor
**111 Places in Atlanta
That You Must Not Miss**
ISBN 978-3-7408-1887-6

Floriana Petersen, Steve Werney
**111 Places in San Francisco
That You Must Not Miss**
ISBN 978-3-7408-2058-9

Laurel Moglen, Julia Posey,
Lyudmila Zotova
**111 Places in Los Angeles
That You Must Not Miss**
ISBN 978-3-7408- 1889-0

Harriet Baskas, Cortney Kelley
**111 Places in Seattle
That You Must Not Miss**
ISBN 978-3-7408-2375-7

Katrina Nattress, Jason Quigley
**111 Places in Portland
That You Must Not Miss**
ISBN 978-3-7408-0750-4

Cristyle Egitto, Jakob Takos
111 Places in Palm Beach
That You Must Not Miss
ISBN 978-3-7408-2398-6

Dana DuTerroil, Joni Fincham,
Daniel Jackson
111 Places in Houston
That You Must Not Miss
ISBN 978-3-7408-2265-1

Dana DuTerroil, Joni Fincham,
Sara S. Murphy
111 Places for Kids in Houston
That You Must Not Miss
ISBN 978-3-7408-2267-5

Kelsey Roslin, Nic Yeager,
Jesse Pitzler
111 Places in Austin
That You Must Not Miss
ISBN 978-3-7408-1642-1

Philip D. Armour, Susie Inverso
111 Places in Denver
That You Must Not Miss
ISBN 978-3-7408-1220-1

Jennifer Bain
111 Places in Ottawa
That You Must Not Miss
ISBN 978-3-7408-1388-8

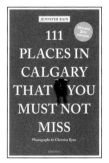

Jennifer Bain, Christina Ryan
111 Places in Calgary
That You Must Not Miss
ISBN 978-3-7408-1559-2

Elizabeth Lenell-Davies,
Anita Genua, Claire Davenport
111 Places in Toronto
That You Must Not Miss
ISBN 978-3-7408-0257-8

David Doroghy, Graeme Menzies
111 Places in Vancouver
That You Must Not Miss
ISBN 978-3-7408-2150-0

Acknowledgements

I have enormous appreciation for the people who gave me ideas, told wondrous stories, and made me laugh.

Many thanks to my editor Karen Seiger for this opportunity, and to photographer John Dean for the fun outings in pursuit of photos. I have so much gratitude for my friends. Diane Baschant and Will Fergusson, my elves, who went with me all over town. To Allison Turner, Edith Obaid Abarca, Wendy McAllister, Rita Golomb, Cecilia Corona, and Jim Sax for your positivity and support.

Warmest thanks to the local National Park Service Rangers who share such a wealth of information, particularly Jeff Reardon and Dana Dierkes, Roger Powell, Katherine Williams, Steve Miller, and Layton Carr for so many Presidential tidbits. Marquette Milton, the first person I spoke with for this book. Joe Swimmer, Susan Gibbs, Brother Sebastian, and Angel Anderson for spectacular tours. Turkish Ambassador Serdar Kiliç, Berkay Altinok, and staff for your generous invitations. Kealy Gordon for your great support at the Smithsonian Institution. Rohulamin Quander, Lorna Grenadier, Anthony Hoston, Summer Knight, and many others for the local lore.
– AMS

Having just wrapped up 111 Places in Baltimore, I wasn't sure I was ready to take the plunge, but once I met Andrea Seiger, I knew I had to be a part of this book too. Her enthusiasm for the District was my guiding light.

I'd like to thank Tom Glasgow of Eastern Market for his kind extension of breakfast hours. As my wife and I approached the counter, he yelled to the back, "Breakfast is OVER!" When we explained why we were there, he lit up and yelled again, "Gimme an order of BLUEBUCKS!" Delicious.

My assistant Penny Forester made a big difference with her maps, grouping locations efficiently so I could make the most of each trip to DC.

Best of all were the times I brought my family along. Ellen is the best navigator, and our son Charlie doesn't mind posing now and then. That's him on the links of the oldest miniature golf course!
– JD

Andrea Seiger is a world and domestic traveler who has lived in Washington DC for over 30 years and has worked in nearly every business involved in tourism and hospitality. When asked how she knows so much about DC her response is usually "because I work in tourism and it is my business to know my city." She lived in Rio de Janeiro, Brazil in the height of the Disco Era, has traveled thousands of miles on the Mayan Route of Mexico and lives to road trip around the Mid-Atlantic US and beyond. Her travel bucket list includes visiting all 50 US States; every country in the continent of the Americas and all of the New 7 Wonders of the World, the Galapagos, Macchu Picchu and Ankor Wat. She is pretty far along on the list. Itchy traveling feet get her out and about as often as possible, whether on the streets of DC or somewhere else in the world.

John Dean is a freelance photographer and video producer, who specializes in photographing people in different environments. He was given a Brownie 620 box camera when he was 7 years old, and he has been hooked ever since. He calls himself an "amateur" in the literal sense that he loves photography and all the doors it has opened for him. He is happy to be working in the current "golden age" of high definition documentary film making, producing videos for the past 15 years for museums and non-profit organizations. He did the photography for *111 Places in Baltimore That You Must Not Miss*.

The information in this book was accurate at the time of publication, but it can change at any time. Please confirm the details for the places you're planning to visit before you head out on your adventures.